THE GLOBE TROTTER IN INDIA

THE GLOBE TROTTER IN INDIA

TWO HUNDRED YEARS AGO

(GEMELLI CARERI)

AND OTHER INDIAN STUDIES

MICHAEL MACMILLAN

ASIAN EDUCATIONAL SERVICES
NEW DELHI ★ MADRAS ★ 1993

ASIAN EDUCATIONAL SERVICES.
* C-2/15, S.D.A. NEW DELHI-110016
* 5 SRIPURAM FIRST STREET, MADRAS-600014.

Price: AES Rs 395 -
First Published: London, 1895
AES Reprint: New Delhi, 1993
ISBN: 81-206-0865-8

Published by J.Jetley
for ASIAN EDUCATIONAL SERVICES
C-2/15, SDA New Delhi-110 016
Processed by Gaurav Jetley
for APEX PUBLICATION SERVICES
New Delhi-110 016
Printed at Gayatri Offset Press
A-66, S. No. 2 Noida, Distt. Ghaziabad (U.P.)

THE

GLOBE TROTTER IN INDIA

TWO HUNDRED YEARS AGO

And Other Indian Studies

BY

MICHAEL MACMILLAN B.A. (OXON.)

Fellow of the Bombay University, and Professor of English Literature at Elphinstone College, Bombay

LONDON

SWAN SONNENSCHEIN & CO.

PATERNOSTER SQUARE

1895

PREFACE

WITH the exception of the paper on Heredity and the Regeneration of India, originally delivered as a lecture to the Elphinstone College Union, the following papers have appeared before in the pages of the *Bombay Gazette*, *Calcutta Review*, and *Madras Christian College Magazine*, the proprietors of which have kindly consented to their republication. The quotations from Gemelli Careri are taken from the translation in *Churchill's Voyages*.

CONTENTS

The Globe Trotter in India Two Hundred Years Ago.

GEMELLI CARERI ON HIS WAY TO INDIA.

GEMELLI CARERI, one of the early European travellers who visited India before the days of the English supremacy, was born at Naples in 1651 and died in 1725. He began his journey round the world, in the course of which he visited India, on June 13th, 1693, and ended it on Dec. 3rd, 1699. Although it was family troubles that drove this Italian doctor in civil law to start on his long journey, he must have had a natural inclination for travelling, as he had already made a tour through Europe in 1683. Before commencing the recital of his travels, he gives his readers some hints as to the various routes to India and as to what the eastern traveller ought to take with him, so that his first chapter might have done very well as an introduction to a seventeenth century Murray's Handbook to India. Of the routes to India available in those days he mentions four. The first was to sail round the Cape in a French, English, Dutch or Portuguese East Indiaman. But by this route there was "much danger to life or at least to health in the midst of these horrible tempests and tedious calms, which keep the spirit in continual alarm, while the body is entirely fed on spoiled food, and one drinks no water which is not tainted and full of worms, all which is due to the sojourn of thirty or forty days that the vessel has to make on the Equator. This voyage may cost from 100 to 200 pieces of eight according to the part of the ship in which you have your berth." The second route was to go by Leghorn or Malta to Alexandria, and thence to sail up the Nile to Cairo, and continue the journey in Mahometan vessels through the Red Sea. The third and commonest route for Europeans was to sail from Leghorn to Alexandretta or Aleppo, and thence proceed to Ispahan by a choice of five caravan routes, all of which, however, were infested with robbers. The fourth and safest route, which Gemelli Careri followed himself and recommended to others, was to go to Constantinople and then on across the Black Sea to Trebizond.

As to the manner of travelling, he recommended those going to the East not to provide themselves with large sums of money or letters of credit, but to travel with merchandise. "The traveller thereby provides himself with a natural means of intercourse with all nations, and even the most barbarous welcome a merchant who brings them the comforts of life, and think that in pillaging or ill-treating him they would offend in his person the right of nations and expose themselves to the same treatment in the form of reprisals." The best merchandise to take to the East would appear at this time to have been the Waterbury watches of the day, and the charms and balms which were the precursors of Holloway's ointment and pills. "One should take these round and long crystals in the shape of an olive made at Venice, because Orientals buy them at a high price to ornament their arms and legs, which they always leave bare. The theriac of Venice is still the most esteemed in the East and at Ispahan. It can easily be bartered for the precious balm of Persia, that is called the balm of the mummy. A large fortune may be gained by making such an exchange with one of the king's eunuchs, for whom it is collected. To make very considerable gain with a small capital and less trouble, it will be necessary to buy at Malta these petrified serpents' tongues and eyes found in the place where St. Paul, according to the common tradition, caused all the venomous animals of the island to assemble and die. They can be bought wholesale at a sou apiece, and in Persia and in India are sold for as much as two crowns, and for much more in China; experience having made plain that the serpents of these countries, however venomous they may be, do no harm to those who wear one of these petrified tongues inside a ring in such a way that the stone touches the flesh. Emeralds sell well, because their colour is extremely pleasing to Mahometans. Cheap watches are in demand there." The traveller is also recommended to provide himself before starting with a certain amount of medical and surgical skill, including, if possible, the ability to operate on diseased eyes. Provided with such knowledge and a medicine box, the traveller was "esteemed and caressed" everywhere in Turkey, Persia, and India, and had the chance of not merely paying his way, but returning home rich by the exercise of the healing art. After this preliminary discourse on choice of route and equipment, Gemelli Careri proceeds to commence the account of his own journey.

On what he saw and did before he began to

travel straight for India we need not dwell. Suffice it to say that he spent some ten months in preliminary travels through Egypt, the Holy Land, and Turkey, before he landed at Trebizond on April 21st, 1694. From Trebizond he went through Asiatic Turkey and Persia, visiting on the way Erzeroum, Kars, Erivan, Ispahan, Shiraz, and finally reaching the Persian Gulf at Bander-Abbas after a land journey of 176 days. On his way through Turkish Asia he met with so much incivility, obstruction, and extortion, that he looked forward to the day when he should cross the border as a release and respite from his troubles. He tells us that, as soon as he got to the further side of the river that parted the Turkish and Persian Empires, he alighted down from his horse to kiss the Persian soil that he had so long yearned to reach in order that he might be delivered from the frauds of the Turks. Persia, however, though an improvement upon Turkey, was not in every respect a traveller's paradise. The officials and people were more courteous to strangers and unbelievers, the caravanserais were all large and magnificent brick buildings, "so uniform and well proportioned, that they are not inferior to the best structures in Europe," but the Shah's messengers had an unpleasant practice of requisitioning travellers' horses for their own use, and the road police exacted continually small fees for the protection they afforded. It is remarkable that not only in Persia but also in Turkey our traveller, though occasionally threatened, was never actually despoiled by highway robbers. Perhaps the horrible punishments inflicted on thieves were sufficiently strong inducements to limit the dishonest to the safer and more profitable employment of petty extortion. Thus it was that not many adventures of an exciting character were encountered on the way. At Erzeroum, owing to a difference of opinion about paying the duty for a gun, a Turk ran after Gemelli with a knife, and would have stabbed him had he not been cleverly collared by Mr. Prescot, an English merchant, who acted as consul in that town. Between Ispahan and Shiraz, one of his travelling companions, the Reverend Father Francis, had to break the head of an obstinate Armenian to settle a disputed charge. But with these exceptions the travellers traversed the whole distance from sea to sea without coming into actual conflict with official or private persons.

Although no sensational adventures are recounted in Gemelli's diary of this journey, it is in other respects full of interest. A traveller through Asia in the seventeenth century was sure to meet strange characters among the religious men and merchants who had left Europe to make their fortunes or preach Christianity in distant countries. Most of his travelling companions were Roman Catholic missionaries. We have seen how one of them gave a specimen of muscular Christianity in a controversy with an Armenian. Another of them was Father Villot, a Lorraine missionary on his way to Erzeroum, who knew the Armenian language perfectly, "and invented a game like that of the goose to make the Armenians remember the divine mysteries, calling it a game of devotion, because the said mysteries were printed on it." The question of the pay and comfort of missionaries, which has lately been discussed with some violence, seems to have already cropped out in the seventeenth century; for Father Dalmasius, as he toiled up the Armenian hills on foot, exclaimed, "Come hither, gentlemen of the Propaganda, and see what a condition we are in here. Come along you who do not give a penny, and I am satisfied you will give all you are worth to be at home again." Among the secular characters whom Gemelli met on his travels, a good specimen of the baser sort was a Frenchman who turned up at Erzeroum on the 8th of May, and "next day became a Mahometan, despairing of ever obtaining his pardon for two duels he fought, killing two men in France." He pretended he had been sent by the French King into Turkey as a spy. As a specimen of the more prosperous adventurer let us take James Norghcamer, Agent of the Dutch Company in Ispahan, whom Gemelli found "shooting turtle doves in the garden which was delicious for its fountains and curious rows of trees. After we had drank merrily, he showed me a dozen horses and mares, the finest any monarch in the world can be master of, as well for mettle as the curious spots of several colours, not inferior to the finest figure, nor could a painter colour them to more perfection. Thence he led me to see his little house of sport, where he had ten hawks fit for all sorts of birds and beasts, with servants to look to them; a custom they have learnt from the Persians, whose greatest delight this is. He had several pipes of gold and silver set with jewels for those to smoke that came to bear him company by his fish pond. In short, he lived great in all respects."

On his way through Persia, Gemelli had the good fortune to be in Ispahan at the time of the death of the Shah, so that he records the funeral ceremonies of one king and the coronation of another. Toward the end of September Scia-Selemon

(Shah Sulaiman) began to have a continual succession of apoplectic fits, and although he distributed 3,700 tomans among the poor and ordered all prisoners to be released, he died on the 29th. The obsequies were performed on the afternoon of August 1st. "An hundred camels and mules led the way, loaded with sweetmeats, and other provisions to be given on the road to a thousand persons that accompanied the body. Then came the body in a large litter, covered with cloth of gold, and carried by two camels led by the king's steward. On the sides went two servants burning the most precious sweets in two fire-pans of gold, and a multitude of Mullahs saying their prayers in a very noisy manner." In such state, surrounded by all the great officials on foot and with their garments rent, the dead body of the king went to the tomb of his ancestors, and the peasants on the way were expected not merely to rend their garments, but also to gash their flesh in token of their grief. The coronation of the new king was by no means an equally imposing ceremony. When the day considered auspicious by the astrologers had arrived, "there was heard an ungrateful sound of drums and trumpets playing to Scia-Ossen (Shah Husain) then seated on the throne, and in this mean manner was the coronation of so great a king solemnised." Five days later Gemelli was at a royal banquet. "First came several sorts of fruit and sweetmeats in golden dishes. Then three great basins of pillau, red, white, and yellow, covered with pullets and other flesh which was distributed in gold plates. I being at the ambassador's table ate no pillau, because I cannot endure butter, and therefore tasted only some fruit seasoned with sugar or vinegar. The king had the same diet on a table covered with cloth of gold." The gold dishes sound grand, but what shall we say of the king's 1,500 horses, "noble creatures with gold troughs before them and great pins of the same metal to tie them by the feet!" At the court were Akbar, son of the Great Mogul, and many ambassadors, including one from the Pope and another from Poland, the latter of whom was trying in vain to rouse the Persians to declare war against Turkey, and so create a diversion in favour of the Eastern European powers then engaged in war with the Ottoman armies. At first it appeared that the new king was something more than an Amurath succeeding an Amurath. Love of drinking had ruined his father in mind and body, and Scia-Ossen signalised his succession by forbidding the use of wine on pain of death, and breaking all the vessels containing wine in the palace. Two poor wretches caught drinking wine were publicly bastinadoed till their nails dropt off, although they pleaded ignorance of the edict. But the hereditary disposition soon proved too strong for his reforming zeal, and before Gemelli left the country Scia-Ossen promised to become as good a toper as his father.

To the antiquarian the most interesting passage in the account of the journey through Persia will be the elaborate description of the palace of Darius at Persepolis, which, owing to the delicacy of the carving and the architectural skill displayed in it, was in Gemelli's opinion such a splendid relic of antiquity, that "there neither is nor ever was a wonder in the world to compare to it." Of more special interest to those of us who live in India is his account of his visit to the Goris, the Zoroastrians who remained in Persia, refusing either to be converted to Mahometanism or to leave their native country. They lived in one long street a mile long, adorned with two rows of green cinar trees. It is interesting to compare their manners and customs as they appeared to an observant traveller in 1694, with the manners and customs of the modern Parsees. They are very careful, he tells us, "to kill all unclean creatures, there being a day in the year appointed on which men and women go about the fields killing the frogs. They drink wine and eat swine's flesh, but it must be bred by themselves and not have eaten anything unclean. They abstain but five days in the year from eating flesh, fish, butter, and eggs, and three other days they eat nothing till night. Besides, they have thirty festivals of their saints. When any of them dies, they carry him out of the town or village to a place wall'd in near the mountain. There they tie the dead body standing upright to a pillar (there being many for the purpose) seven spans high; and going to prayers for the soul of the person departed, they stand till the crows come to eat the body; if they begin with the right eye, they bury the body and return home joyfully, looking upon it as a good omen; if they fall upon the left eye, they go away disconsolate, leaving the body unburied." The whole account of the Goris deserves to be examined carefully by the Parsees of to-day, and, if so examined, will be a good test passage by which to form an opinion of the general accuracy or inaccuracy of Gemelli's narrative.

GEMELLI CARERI IN THE PERSIAN GULF AND INDIAN OCEAN.

It was at Bander Congo that Gemelli Careri first found himself within the sphere of Indian influence. Indeed, Bander Congo might also be regarded as a part of Portuguese India, so great were the powers and privileges granted to the Portuguese in this port. There they received by treaty from the king of Persia a tribute of five horses and eleven hundred tomans a year. There they had their flag flying and exercised jurisdiction over all Christians in the town, and we are even told that their predominance was so great that no Christian could be converted to Mahometanism there. Indeed, in the words of our author, they had "almost as absolute a command as if they were in Goa, not only over their own subjects, but all Christians who passed that way."

At the time of his arrival the Hindu merchants were adorning their houses inside and out with fine cloth and lamps for the Diwali. They received the stranger hospitably, and after sprinkling him with rose-water entertained him with an exhibition of Indian dancers. This account of what he saw is interesting as being, perhaps, the first description of an Indian nautch by an European pen, although the performance has been so often described by Western travellers to the East since his time. The dancing women were "clothed some in Persian, others in Indian dress, and sang in both languages. The former had a dress of striped silk which did not reach lower than the calf of the leg and widened below like a petticoat. Underneath they had a long pair of drawers which descended to the instep and were ornamented with a circlet of silver. They had also a large number of gold and silver rings on their toes and fingers which were painted with *imma* or red earth, as also their teeth, the inside of their eyes, and their foreheads were with black earth. They wore a little cap bordered with a band of gauze, half silk and half thread, whence fell their long hair down to their waists. A long yellow and red veil covered their shoulders and came eddying as far as their arms. Besides double earrings they had in the middle of their nostrils a great gold ring, and other pendants fastened or glued to their foreheads. But of all these ornaments the most uncomfortable seemed to me to be a stud gilt or of gold which they passed through and through the curved part at the top of the nose, which appeared to us Europeans a great deformity. They had a gold carcanet or a collar of pearls, according to their means, and beautiful bracelets. In this dress they began to dance with much gravity to the sound of a drum and of two pieces of metal, together with the bells they had on their feet. Afterwards they excited themselves by a thousand gestures and a thousand immodest postures, cracking their fingers with much grace and from time to time mingling songs with the dance, which pleased me so much that I wished to see them more than once, and others also who danced in a different manner in another house."

While Gemelli Careri was staying at Bander Congo, the town was startled by a characteristic Oriental tragedy. The Persian custom-house officer, being displeased with the conduct of two rich Arab merchants, took advantage of a visit they paid him to poison them with diamond dust, which he put in their cups of coffee. One of them drank the coffee, but the other courteously gave his cup to the uncle of the Persian official. Both of those who drank the poisoned coffee died in agony on the following night. The servant who had prepared the coffee disappeared, and it was said that he had been killed for fear he might reveal his master's crime.

At Bander Congo our traveller was first introduced to the practices of the Hindu religion. While there, he visited under a great banyan tree two Hindu temples, and saw the Indian settlers on the Persian coast taking their offerings of rice and butter to the silver-headed and silver-footed image of Bhawani. Every morning and evening they went to the seashore to scatter rice on the water for the benefit of the fishers and to bring back water to wash the face and ears of their families. The Indian merchants in Persia made their best profit out of pearls. Gemelli saw them separating the large from the small ones by passing them through copper sieves as if they were making shot. By taking them to Surat they could make thirty per cent. gain, if they managed to smuggle them in without being detected by the custom-house officers there.

In spite of the nautches, the shooting and the Roman Catholic services that Gemelli enjoyed at Bander Congo, he was eager to go on to India. His friends, Father Francis and Father Constantine, had taken passages for themselves and for their slaves on an English ship bound for Surat, and wanted him to accompany them. But he would not embark on an English vessel, fearing the rigorous custom-house at Surat and the French who lay in wait for English ships attempting to enter that harbour. So he preferred a Moorish ship which was taking to Damaun eight horses that the king of Portugal had received as tribute from the king of Persia. Although he got his passage for nothing, he had good reason to repent of his choice before he reached his destination.

He got on board at five o'clock on a Friday night. As ships were not allowed to supply themselves with water at Bander Congo for fear of a water famine there, they touched at Angon, but, finding the cisterns there dry, had to go on two miles further to the island of Kechini, where they took in a supply of brackish water. Gemelli landed on the island to shoot and take notes, and found that the inhabitants knew how to manufacture the dried fish familiar to us under the name of Bombay ducks. "They eat there excellent pilchards, as also in the island of Angon. The people of the country have no better food. They have them dried in the sun and keep them as substitutes for bread during the whole year. Fine pearls are also obtained in these two islands, but the islanders like their pilchards better, as something more sure and easy to fish." On the first of December he sailed past Ormuz. Nothing remained to give evidence of the ancient wealth which won its immortality in Milton's sounding verse. "It grows neither tree nor herb, being all covered with very white salt which causes its barrenness. The water which falls from heaven is the only sweet water to be got for drinking there, and it is collected in cisterns for the garrison of the fort."

Gemelli evidently kept a diary on his voyage, extracts from which we will endeavour to construct out of his detailed narrative, taking care to add nothing, but abridging and omitting when convenient.

Dec. 4th.—Entered Indian Ocean without losing sight of land. The Moors continually occupied in rubbing their eyelids with a black drug, good, they say, for the eyes, pulling out with little pincers the hair of their beards where they don't want them to grow again, and covering the nails of their feet and hands with red earth. They are, however, much less insolent in their behaviour to strangers than the Turks. The captain and crew pay me much respect on account of the recommendation of the Superintendent of Bander Congo.

Dec. 7th.—Becalmed before uninhabited islands, used as retreats by corsairs. Excessively hot. Indian winter seems like an Italian summer. The Persians on board early in the morning strip themselves naked and throw plenty of salt water over their heads. At evening a favourable wind took us in sight of the island of Pishini. Our head still to the east, in order that after making the point of Diu we may sail more easily towards Surat and Damaun.

Dec. 8th.—False alarm. Vessel coming to meet us. Amused to see the eagerness with which the Moors take their rusty matchlocks on which they base their hopes of defence, as the ship has only eight cannon, bad and worse served. The ship sheers off, showing a red flag in token of amity.

Dec. 9th.—At daybreak a ship in the east. The Moors so frightened that, taking their arms, they begin to howl like dogs barking at a distance. They won't get into the skiff to board the vessel, as I advise them to do, offering myself to go with them. Presently the suspicious vessel sails away northwards and puts an end to the cries and fears of the Moors, who thought it was one of the corsairs, called Sangans, inhabiting the isles and marshy places on the continent near Sind and Gujarat.

In the evening a calm. Saw a Terrankin or ship of Kanas. We had some reason to fear that it might take advantage of the darkness of night to surprise us, so I advised the captain to give powder and shot to twenty soldiers who were on board, and to have the artillery loaded and set sentinels; for the Moors travel like brutes without any foresight, waiting for the enemy to be upon them before they distribute ammunition and load.

Dec. 10th.—The terrankin out of sight.

Dec. 11th.—An annoying calm. In the evening a sailor caught a fish weighing five pounds. As it was the first caught on the voyage, the sailors put it up to auction, according to the custom of the Moors, and fastened it to the mast. After a brisk competition a merchant bought it for twenty-two abasis (about six crowns), which were divided among the sailors for a dinner.

Dec. 12th and 13th.—Contrary winds. Changed our course to avoid a boat supposed to be manned by Sangans. At night, real danger in the form of a squall.

Dec. 14th.—Squall worse and wind contrary. The ignorant sailors resolve to return to Kechini, although we see an English vessel keeping steadily on her course. In vain I encouraged them and assured them that the tempest would not last. They would not be persuaded. However, I had prophesied truly: the storm stopped before night, and we returned to our course, the captain swearing that it was for love of me that he turned the ship's head eastward.

Saw for the first time the flying fish. It rises a gun shot above the water and falls back again, its wings being unable to sustain its weight of ten or twelve ounces. It quits its natural element when pursued by the fish called by the Portuguese the abnous. This fish, which eats the others, is blue, of good flavour, and enough for four persons.

Dec. 15th.—A furious wind. We are in danger. A tremendous fall of rain all night, wetting those below as well as those on deck. The Moorish women in the cabin under the poop weep bitterly, while their husbands on deck call upon Mahomet to save them from the death which they think near.

Dec. 16th.—Fine weather again. The sailors think they descry the continent at Giaske which belongs to the Baluchis, and we make for it, but can't regain what we lost the day before. All this was due to the incredible ignorance of the pilot who came at a venture, and at Congo had never been anything but a tobacconist. The captain, who saw the danger to which we were exposed by the pilot's inexperience, addressed a long discourse to me and told me that I ought to take charge of the ship. I excused myself, and told him that the old pilot, after having chewed opium all day to add to the imbecility due to old age, sailed through the night with the two topsails lowered and the head of the ship towards the land, thereby exposing the ship to the danger of running into rocks. If the captain wished to save us from perishing, he must spread all sail and turn the ship's head to sea. He immediately gave orders to this effect, and prayed me to attend to the compass and watch over the management of the ship, because, in addition to the fact that he no longer had confidence in the ignorant pilot, he believed that I understood navigation and naval charts. As the danger was common, I yielded to the captain's prayer, conducted the working of the ship, and made the soldiers take their arms when any ship appeared in sight. So that on the slightest occasion they immediately call for the *Aga Gemelli*, maintaining that as an European I ought to know everything—so high is the opinion they have of us. Thus they make me play the part both of commander and pilot. However, as I don't know much more than them, all that I do is to guide the ship southward during the day. As sleep is a necessity, at night I leave the direction to the ignorant pilot, who robs us of all the progress made during the day.

Dec. 17th.—The result is that, though we spread five sails and had a good wind, we find ourselves in the same place as we were in eleven days ago.

Such are the delays to which those are exposed who embark on Moorish vessels. Towards evening we sight some towns in the kingdom of Sind, a province of the Great Mogul.

Dec. 25th.—I have such a quarrel with the pilot, who did not work the ship at all during the night, that I refuse any more to have anything to do with the working of the ship.

Dec. 28th.—At daybreak the ignorant sailors and pilot think they have made out the town and fortress of Diu, which projects into the sea more than any other. On this glad tidings the captain distributes to all the crew, according to the Moorish custom, *cacciari,* which is a mixture of black beans, rice, and lentils. They eat it in Indian fashion, dipping one hand in a plate of melted butter and filling it in another plate with the cacciari, which they carry to the mouth by handfuls.

The sailors turn out to have been mistaken. Having recognised their error, they turn the ship's head towards the south for Damaun in such a way that the wind, from being contrary, becomes favourable.

Dec. 29th.—I have already said that the pilot understood neither the compass nor charts. This was how it happened that to-day, seeing themselves near land, they all persuaded themselves that it was the village of Maym (Mahim?) near Bassein, a town belonging to the Portuguese, and therefore they had arrived at the end of their voyage. All the crew manifested great joy, and still more the merchants, who believed that they had saved their persons and their goods. As for the ignorant pilot, proud of having conducted the ship so successfully to India, he went round with a paper in his hand to mark down what the passengers promised him for having shown such diligence. When he came to me, I told him I would give him nothing, because I knew well that the land we saw was not what he thought it was.

Gemelli's suspicions turned out to be well founded. When they landed they found to their alarm that, instead of being at Mahim, they were at Mangalore in Gujarat, 400 miles north-east of Damaun. However, after that they got on rather better, and on January 8th, 1695, our traveller found himself, to his great joy, actually anchored off Damaun, after a voyage of 1,200 miles, which would have been only half as long if they had had an efficient pilot.

GEMELLI CARERI IN PORTUGUESE INDIA.

The farther Gemelli was from his native land, the better he was pleased. We have seen how he kissed the Persian soil as soon as he passed the boundary line between the Turkish and Persian Empires. His emotions of delight seem to have been even stronger when he landed at last on the strand of India. "A traveller," he remarks, "who has been long separated from his native land, and who has suffered all kinds of fatigues, does not feel greater joy at returning home and finding himself surrounded by his friends, to whom he tells what he has seen, than that which I felt on arriving at India after a very wearisome voyage. The pleasure belonging to the mere recital of all the precious things produced by this rich country may indicate the great satisfaction I enjoy at this moment, when I am on the point of seeing them and forming an opinion of them for myself."

Damaun, the first town in India that he made the acquaintance of, did not fall beneath his expectations. When he landed, he found himself in a very beautiful town built in Italian style and divided by large parallel streets. The houses were tiled, and each was surrounded by its own garden planted with fruit trees. The windows, instead of glass, were fitted with oyster shells so beautifully prepared that they were transparent. Gemelli was very much impressed with the grandeur of the Portuguese in Damaun, whether he looked to their tables, their garments, or the number of slaves who carried them about—even the friars—in richly ornamented palanquins. For amusement they indulged in hunting boars, wolves, foxes, hares, and tigers. About tigers and boars Gemelli was told at Damaun a strange piece of natural history which we may believe or not, according to the amount of our credulity. "As the tigers," we read, "are always going on the tracks of the boars, these latter, taught by nature to defend themselves, roll in the mud and then dry themselves in the sun until it has made them a very hard crust. In this way, instead of becoming the prey of their enemies, it often happens that they tear them with their sharp pointed tusks, having the whole time to kill them that the tigers are engaged in digging their claws into this mud to tear it." Gemelli was rather particular about his food, and found nothing very good to eat in Damaun, except the bread and the fruits. The beef and pork were bad, and sheep and goats were seldom killed. The necessity of strict abstemiousness was generally recognised.

Any intemperance was sure to be punished by terrible attacks of disease, incurable, or that could only be cured by such violent burning of the body that those who recovered bore the scars of the hot iron upon them till their dying day. The dread of these diseases, and, still more, of the remedies, ought to have been a sufficient deterrent from excessive indulgence in the pleasures of the table.

From Damaun Gemelli visited Surat, at that time the principal port in India, "all nations in the world trading thither, no ship sailing the Indian Ocean but what puts in there to buy, sell, or load." All its wealth of spices, cottons, silk, gold stuffs, muslins, agates, etc., was defended only by a weak wall, and the streets were narrow, and the houses were made of mud. Gemelli only stayed a few days there, and does not give a detailed description of the city.

The next town he visited was Bassein, still in its glory as a great Indo-European city, although destined to be wrested from the Portuguese forty-three years later, after having been in their possession for more than two centuries. What Gemelli admired most at Bassein was the Cassabo, a great pleasure ground fifteen miles long, full of delightful gardens planted with all kinds of Indian fruit trees, and kept green and fruitful by continual watering :

"so that the gentry, allured by the cool and delightful walks, all have their pleasure-houses at Cassabo, to go thither in the hottest weather to take the air and get away from the contagious and pestilential disease called Carazzo that infects all the cities of the northern coast." Our traveller attended a wedding of some people of quality at Bassein, and, wondering that the bridegroom gave the bride his left hand, was told that such was the Portuguese custom, the idea being to leave the bridegroom's right hand free to defend his bride. Gemelli had himself a tempting offer of marriage at Bassein. He was a Doctor of Civil Law, and there was no Portuguese Doctors of Civil Law in India. So, as an inducement to keep him in the country, he was offered as wife a lady with a portion of 20,000 pieces of eight (Rs. 44,000), and was promised legal work that would bring him in 600 pieces of eight (Rs. 1,320) a year. Having no inclination to live in those hot climates, he answered that, though offered 100,000 pieces of eight, he would never be induced to quit Europe forever. Whether the lady was of prepossessing appearance or not is a point upon which our curiosity is not satisfied.

From Bassein Gemelli made an expedition to the Buddhist caves at Kennery, twenty miles from

Bombay on the island of Salsette. As neither Tavernier nor any other European traveller had described them before him, he gives a long and elaborate account of their architectural features. We must not expect to get from him valuable historical information about their origin. He lived in an age not famous for minute historical investigation: so, hearing that the construction of the caves was ascribed to Alexander the Great, he accepts the statement with simple faith on account of the "extraordinary and incomparable workmanship, which certainly could be undertaken by none but Alexander." The Greek conqueror seems to have been found as useful in India as the Devil in England, when an author had to be found for great works of unknown origin. Thus the cutting of a way through the rock for the Tanna creek was also attributed to him. No doubt the two conjectures supported each other, and were regarded as conclusive evidence of Alexander's presence as far south as Bassein. So, Gemelli was quite satisfied and did not trouble his head to question the received belief about the construction of the caves, but devoted all his energies to giving a full description of them, which is too long to be here reproduced. Anyone can nowadays visit them from Bombay with very little exertion. Only it is to be hoped that few who visit the caves may have their inner man as ill fortified for the expedition as Gemelli's was. Landing hot and dry on the island of Salsette, he was offered by Father Edward, to whose hospitality he had been recommended, nothing more sustaining than a glass of water and two preserved citron peels, which were so covered with ants that he could only eat one. On the following day, when he was starting early for the caves, the same Father Edward told him the bread was not baked yet, and that he could dine in a village half way. When he got to the village indicated, he found nothing to eat there but a little half-boiled rice and water, so he went on his way fasting. That he was able on an empty stomach to make such a thorough investigation of the caves as he did reflects great credit on his energy and perseverance. It is sad to relate that, when he returned to Father Edward's roof after his labours, he fared little better, and "went to bed, quite spent with hunger and weariness, wishing for the next day that he might fly from that wretched place." Perhaps, if Gemelli had been more hospitably treated in Salsette, he might have ventured on to Bombay and told us how it looked in 1695. Unfortunately he did not choose to do so, but went straight back to his friends at Bassein.

Gemelli next visited Goa, the metropolis of Portuguese India. Here he saw most plainly the evidence of the decline of Portuguese power in India, which he attributed chiefly to the hostility of the Dutch, and to the fact that the conquest of Brazil diverted the greater portion of Portuguese energy to the New World. The effect of these causes was visible in the decline of Goa from its former greatness, manifested by the compass of its walls, which extended full four leagues, with good bastions and redoubts, a world too wide for the city of some 20,000 inhabitants that Gemelli visited in 1695. He found its trade declining, and its wealth and grandeur impaired "to such a degree that it was reduced to a miserable condition." The commencement of the decline of Goa was supposed to have been indicated seventy-four years before Gemelli's arrival by a crucifix on a hill in Goa which "was found with its back miraculously turned towards Goa, which city from that time has very much declined." There was another miraculous crucifix in the church of St. Monica's Augustinian nuns, one of whom had died in the monastery "with the reputation of sanctity, she having the signs of our Saviour's wounds found upon her, and on her head, as it were, the goring of thorns, whereof the archbishop took authentic information." But, of course, the greatest object of religious veneration at Goa was the body of St. Francis Xavier at the church of Bon-Jesu. Gemelli, as a great favour, was allowed to view it, although for nine years past the Jesuits had allowed it to be seen only by the Viceroy and some other persons of quality. It was in a crystal coffin, within another of silver, on a pedestal of stone; but they expected a noble tomb of porphyry stone from Florence, ordered to be made by the Great Duke. Gemelli tells us that "since, with the Pope's leave, the saint's arm was cut off, the rest of the body has decayed, as if he had resented it." It was on account of this supposed resentment that the Jesuits were unwilling to show the body to everybody who wanted to see it.

Of the European nations in India, Gemelli evidently much preferred the Portuguese to the Dutch and English, which preference is natural enough, as he was a zealous Roman Catholic. He specially commends Portuguese politeness. "Courteous," he remarks, "is the Portuguese nation," and elsewhere he speaks of "the Portuguese civility, which in all places I found they practised more towards me than towards their own countrymen." One good story he tells that shows how the Portuguese occasionally abused their knowledge of the ceremonial law of etiquette, and how an Indian prince outwitted them. The son of an Indian king about to visit a Portuguese Governor got an inkling that an attempt would be made to sit upon him by giving him no chair to sit upon: so he gave to two slaves instructions of such a kind that he both avoided the affront and effectually turned the tables on the Portuguese magnate. "Being come into the Governor's room, and seeing no chair brought him, he caused his two slaves to squat down, and sat upon them. The Portuguese admired his ingenuity, and presently ordered chairs to be brought. After the visit the two slaves stayed in the Governor's house, and their master being told of it by the Governor's servants, that he might call them away, he answered he did not use to carry away the chairs he sat on." The Indian prince's ingenuity in converting his slaves into chairs rivals that of the Highland chief who won a bet with an English lord by turning his tall retainers into candlesticks, as related in Scott's *Marquis of Montrose.*

A VISIT TO THE GREAT MOGUL.

Gemelli only made one expedition into the interior of India, but what he saw at the end of his short journey is of considerable interest to the historian. He started on March 5th, 1694, from Goa to visit Aurangzebe's camp at Galgala. His journey there and back was very uncomfortable, for he tells us "it is far different travelling through the Mogul's country than through Persia or Turkey, for there are no beasts for carriage to be found, nor caravanserais at convenient distances, nor provisions; and, what is worse, there is no safety from thieves. He, therefore, that has not a horse of his own must mount upon an ox; and besides that inconveniency must carry along with him his provisions and utensils to dress it, rice, pulse, and meal being only to be found in great towns inhabited by the Mogulstans. At night the clear sky will be all a man's covering or else a tree." He acknowledges, however, that these remarks are only applicable to the neighbourhood of Beejapoor, which was then the battle-field of India, and harassed by continual war. In the northern parts of the Empire, near Surat or Ahmedabad, travelling was safer and more comfortable. He started, as we have seen, on March 5th, employing three natives to carry his luggage, whom he kept up to the mark by a liberal use of his cudgel, "because they will never do good service either for fair words or money, but run away as soon as they can, and on the other side when thrashed they load themselves like asses." On the 7th, not far from Portuguese territory, he saw the dismal spectacle of a *sati*. The victim "being come to the place appointed went about undaunted, taking leave of them all; after which she was laid all along with her head on a block in a cottage twelve spans square made of small wood wet with oil, but bound to a stake that she might not run away with the fright of the fire Lying in this posture, chewing betel, she asked of the standers-by whether they had any business by her to the other world, and having received several gifts and letters from those ignorant people to carry to their dead friends, she wrapped them up in a cloth. This done, the Brahman who had been encouraging her came out of the hut and caused it to be fired, the friends pouring vessels of oil on her that she might be the sooner reduced to ashes and out of pain." Such sights were ordinary incidents of a journey through India two hundred years ago.

In spite of the difficulties and dangers of the journey, which latter must have been considerably enhanced by his practice of breaking idols whenever he thought he could do so unobserved, our traveller managed to reach his destination on March 17th. He was hospitably received by the leading Christians serving in Aurangzebe's army. They told him it was a pleasure and diversion to serve the Great Mogul, because no prince paid his soldiers better, and, if they did not choose to fight and keep guard properly, they were only punished by losing their pay for the day they were convicted of such dereliction of duty. They were also not deprived of the consolations of religion by their bigoted employer. The Roman Catholics in the army had a convenient chapel with mud walls in which two Canarese priests officiated. The Christian officers were allowed to enforce strict discipline. Gemelli saw two Mahomedans convicted of being drunk bound to a stake and cruelly lashed for their offence by order of a Christian captain, whom they humbly thanked for inflicting upon them such a salutary chastisement. The whole number of the forces in the camp was estimated to amount to 60,000 horse, and a million foot soldiers, for whose baggage there were 50,000 camels and 3,000 elephants. Taking into account the camp-followers, merchants, artisans and other non-combatants, Gemelli described the whole camp as a "moving city containing five million souls and abounding not only in provisions but in all things that could be desired." We are not told how much space was occupied by this huge assemblage, but everything was on a vast scale. The Emperor's and princes' tents occupied an enclosure three miles in compass, defended by palisades, ditches, and five hundred falconets.

On the 21st of March, Gemelli had the honour of being admitted by the great Emperor to a private audience. The imperial tents were surrounded by an outer or inner court which had to be passed before getting into the presence of the Emperor. In the outer court Gemelli saw kettle-drums and other musical instruments, and a gold ball between two gilt hands, which was carried by elephants on the march as the imperial ensign. In the second inner court was the durbar-tent. Passing through this, Gemelli found himself in the presence of the Emperor, who was seated on rich carpets and gold-embroidered cushions. Aurangzebe asked him what country he belonged to, why he had come, and whether he wished to enter the imperial service. To this Gemelli answered full courteously that he had come to the camp "only out of curiosity to see the greatest monarch in Asia, as his majesty was, and the grandeur of his court and army." The Emperor next asked him questions about the war in Hungary between the Turks and the European powers, and then dismissed him, as it was time for the public audience. Gemelli attended the public audience too. The Emperor came in, leaning on a staff forked at the top, and took his seat on a gilt throne. He had a white turban tied with a gold web and ornamented by one very large emerald surrounded by four smaller ones. Two servants warded off the flies with long white horse-tails, and another stood with a green umbrella to protect him against the sun. In person he was "of a low stature, with a large nose, slender, and stooping with age. The whiteness of his round beard was more visible on his olive-coloured skin." Although he was now seventy-eight years old, he endorsed petitions with his own hand, writing without the help of spectacles, and from his cheerful smiles he seemed to take pleasure in his work. While the audience was going on, there was a review of the elephants, that the Emperor might see if the omrahs to whom they were entrusted kept them in good condition. After this the princes of the blood royal, including the Emperor's great-grandson, came in, clothed in silk vests adorned with precious stones and gold collars. After paying their obeisance by putting their hands to the ground, on their heads, and on their breasts, they sat down on the first floor of the throne on the left. The picture of the old Emperor with a benevolent smile on his countenance, and his children and grandchildren clustered round his throne, is delightfully suggestive of domestic felicity. It is a pity to mar it by thinking of the many deeds of blood against his own kindred by which he obtained and established his throne. He knew that it was the hereditary practice of his dynasty for the son to rebel against the father. He therefore blamed the folly of his father, Shah Jehan, who prepared the way for his own overthrow by giving the command of his armies to his sons, although he "might have learnt by many years' experience that the kings of Hindustan, when they grow old, must keep at the head of a powerful army to defend themselves against their sons." Gemelli prophesied that, notwithstanding all his precautions, he would come to no better an end than his predecessors, but history has not verified the prediction.

Next to the Emperor himself, the most interesting person that Gemelli saw at Galgala was Sicunder Adil Shah, the deposed king of Beejapoor, who went to the royal tent to pay his respects with a handsome retinue. "He was a sprightly youth, twenty-nine years of age, of a good stature, and olive-coloured complexion." His capital had been taken by the army of Aurangzebe in 1686, and, according to Meadows Taylor, he died in captivity three years after. But Gemelli relates that he saw him alive at Galgala in 1695. King Tanak Shah of Golcondah, who had lost his throne and liberty about a year after the fall of Beejapoor, was not with the Emperor at Galgala, but imprisoned in the fortress of Dowlutabad. Gemelli heard interesting details of the fall of Golcondah from European officers in the Mogul army who had taken part in the campaign.

At Galgala Gemelli was unfortunately deserted by his interpreter and other attendants: so he was reduced to the painful necessity of proceeding on his return journey without any servant, and had "to venture all alone through a country infested with robbers and enemies to Christianity." He started on Sunday, March 27th, after first hearing mass at the mud-built chapel in Aurangzebe's camp. He had great difficulty in getting eatable food on the way. On the second day of his journey, he writes: "Desiring a Gentile by signs to make me a cake of bread, the knave, instead of wheaten flour, made it of *načhini*, which is a black seed that makes a man giddy, and so ill-tasted that a dog would not eat it. Whilst it was hot, necessity made me eat that bread of sorrow; but I could not swallow it cold though I had none for three days." Trees and bushes afforded him shelter by night. On April 2nd he was stopped by Mahrattas, who inquired of him by signs whether he could shoot a musket or cannon. On his replying in the negative they let him go. The hardships he encountered on this journey were so great that when he got back to Goa on April 5th he was very ill. His friends in that city, who had tried to dissuade him from making the expedition into the interior, were not surprised that he returned in such sorry plight. "The Father Prefect, seeing me so sick, told me that had happened because I would not take his advice. I answered '*Heu patior telis vulnera facta meis.*' Both he and Father Hippolitus endeavoured to recover me with good fowls, to which the best sauce was their kindness; and thus I recovered my flitting spirits."

GEMELLI CARERI AND HIS TIMES.

We do not propose to follow the footsteps of our seventeenth century globe-trotter on the rest of his journey round the world. Naturally our interest in him diminishes when he sails away from the port of Goa to travel farther east. Yet from a more universal point of view his travels are interesting to the end. From Goa he sailed to Macao, on the way passing by the islands of Ceylon and Sumatra and making a short stay at Malacca. From Macao he made a seven months' tour in China, visiting the great cities of Canton, Nanking and Peking, and personally inspecting the Great Wall of China. He was graciously admitted to an interview by the Emperor of China, as he had been in India by the Great Mogul. From China he sailed to Manilla, and then across the Pacific, which he did not find at all pacific, to Acapulco. He stayed nearly eleven months in Mexico, visiting the principal cities, travelling through the country and risking his life in dangerous descents into the bowels of the earth to see the silver mines. In the end of the year 1698 he took ship on board the *Sevilian*, joined the Spanish plate fleet at Havana, and sailed with it across to Cadiz. Finally he concluded, in December 1699, at Naples, his voyage round the world, in which he had spent five years five months and twenty days of his life.

It does not take so long to get round the world now. Gemelli believed many strange things; but if he had been told that in two hundred years it would be possible to make the circuit of the world in eighty days, he would have been inclined to laugh in the face of his informant. It took Gemelli more then eighty days to sail across the Atlantic to Cadiz, and his voyage through the Pacific from Manilla to Acapulco extended to over twenty-nine weeks. So that in his time it was not advisable for any one who had not a very large amount of spare time at his disposal to undertake a journey round the world. The account given of the hard and disgusting fare obtainable on this long voyage across the Pacific might be read with advantage by luxurious travellers of the present day, who are ready to grumble if their dinners at sea are not quite such as are supplied by the best hotel on land. Gemelli made arrangements with the boatswain to supply him with food. On flesh days he got "*tassajos fritos,*" that is, steaks of beef and buffalo dried in the sun or wind, "which are so hard that it is impossible to eat them without they are first well beaten like stockfish, nor is there any digesting them without the help of a purge." On fish days he had rotten fish and vegetables like kidney beans full of maggots that swam on the top of the broth. The only variety of diet was when they happened to catch sharks. The biscuits were also full of maggots. If such was the diet available for a passenger who could pay for what he wanted, the lot of the poor sailors must have been much worse, cheated as they were of their provisions by the master of the ship. The sailors had to be paid well for undertaking such a voyage, or they would never have been tempted to embark. They got three hundred and fifty pieces of eight (Rs. 770) for the return voyage. The merchants made profits at the rate of 150 to 200 per cent. It was reckoned that the captain of Gemelli's ship would make forty thousand pieces of eight by the voyage and the pilot twenty thousand.

The amusements they had on boardship, besides the shark fishing, were dancing and occasional acting. On December 7th, 1697, although a sailor had died in the morning, the crew celebrated saturnalia like those that used to be, and perhaps are still, indulged in by sailors on the occasion of crossing the line. Mock courts were established to try the officers and passengers. "The clerk read every man's indictment, and then the judges passed sentence of death, which was immediately bought off, with money, chocolate, sugar, biscuit, flesh, sweetmeats, wine, and the like. The best of it was that he who did not pay immediately, or give good security, was laid on with a rope's end at the least sign given by the president." Gemelli was something of a gourmand, so we are not surprised to find that the charge brought against him was eating too much of the fish called *cachorretas*. In spite of such casual diversions the voyage was terribly long and tedious, and the first signs of approaching land were looked for as eagerly as by Columbus and his sailors when they crossed the Atlantic. When the first seaweed was seen, the sailor who saw it got a chain of gold from the captain and fifty pieces of eight from the passengers. At the same time a bell was rung at the prow, everybody congratulated everybody else to the sound of drums and trumpets, and the *Te Deum* was sung. Nor are these rejoicings wonderful when we consider the length and hardship of the voyage on the one hand, and the great profit expected at the end of the voyage on the other.

On land Gemelli suffered less comfort and incurred less danger than might have been expected. His last days in Europe were spent in chains, into which he had been thrown on suspicion of being a Venetian spy. But in none of the other three Continents did he suffer the indignity of imprisonment. Although he was subject to a great deal of petty extortion, he was never robbed of the bulk of his possessions, which cannot have been small, as he carried with him some merchandise and collected curiosities in the countries he went through. Also he carried with him to the end the MSS. of his travels, which he seems to have written carefully every day. We have seen that he found Persia well supplied with commodious caravanserais. In India he was hospitably entertained in the Portuguese cities as a good Roman Catholic, but fared worse when he penetrated into the interior. In the interior of China travelling was remarkably safe. At intervals of four miles along the canals guards were stationed, armed with firelocks, and they had large boats, with cannons in the prow, ready to pursue robbers. Similar care was taken to defend the roads. He was luxuriously rowed along the canals in boats, and it was "very pleasant travelling, both the green banks appearing as a man lies in his bed." Pheasants and fowls and hares were extremely cheap. At one place he bought four pheasants for two shillings and hares at three halfpence a piece. In Mexico there were travellers' bungalows provided with two servants—one to order the traveller whatever he might require, the other (a messman) to cook his food and supply him with fuel and water, all at the public expense Gemelli was very particular about his inner man, and informs his readers of the fact as often as he was incommoded by bad or insufficient food. On the whole he seems to have fared pretty well. As to his outer man, we know that on the way through

Persia he was clad in buckskin breeches, on which account his fellow-travellers amused themselves by pretending that he was a wrestler, as the Persian wrestlers wore such garments. When those who saw him thought he was too lean for wrestling, they were told he was grown lean owing to excessive exercise. By the time he reached China his buckskin breeches were presumably worn out, for we find him dressed in Chinese clothes.

What strikes us most, perhaps, when we attempt by the help of Gemelli's travels to estimate the progress made by the world in the last two hundred years, is his great credulity. In this respect there is far less difference between him and Herodotus, who lived more than two thousand years before him, than between him and an ordinary nineteenth century traveller. We have no reason to think that Gemelli was exceptionally credulous for his age. He was an educated man, and as a Doctor of Civil Law must have had some practice in sifting evidence. His frequent criticisms of Tavernier show that he knew well enough that travellers were in danger of being misled by the deceitfulness of their informants or by misunderstanding. Yet he was ready to accept numberless statements that no educated man of the present day would think worthy of a moment's consideration. Many instances of his credulity have already been mentioned incidentally, but plenty more are to be found scattered over his pages. He took away from Egypt a mummy's skull, "being good, as they say, for wounds and some distempers," and this treasure he carried all round the world with him. He thoroughly believed in the active interposition of the devil in the affairs of the world. Seeing some Arabians striking their breasts with iron pins heavy enough to drive through a wall and not hurting themselves, he remarks: "How this came to pass they best know and the devil that teaches them; but this I know, that these cheats and sons of perdition would not suffer another to strike them with the same pin, for then perhaps the charm would have failed them." An Indian tumbler at Bassein performed such wonderful feats as could not be done, Gemelli thought, without some supernatural assistance. Speaking of some of the inhabitants of the Philippine Islands, he remarks gravely that "the devil appears to some of them because they call upon him in time of need and offer sacrifice to him." He accounts for the number of blind people in Bengal by the custom of exposing infants at night to be pecked at by crows. He accepts with faith the story of an old man at Diu who lived to over 400. "He had changed his teeth three times, and his beard as often grew grey after having been black." Compared with him, the old lady of 114 in the last American census may hide her diminished head. We have seen the immense estimate Gemelli formed of the number of the Mogul's army at Galgala. Still more astonishing is the population he attributes to the great cities of China, though not without hesitation, on the authority of Roman Catholic missionaries, who estimated the population of Peking at 16,000,000 and of Nanking at 32,000,000! In the Philippine Islands he saw leaves which, "when they come to a certain pitch of ripeness, become living creatures with wings, feet and tail, and fly like any bird, though they remain of the same colour as the other leaves." What he saw were, no doubt, specimens of those insects which by the process of natural selection have become almost indistinguishable from their leafy habitat. Among the many wonderful herbs, he mentions a nut which was such an effective antidote against poison that, if you carried it about your person, it not only protected you but hurt your would-be poisoner. "This is so certain," we are told, "that Father Alexius, a Jesuit, having one of these nuts he found accidentally in the garden in his pocket, and an Indian coming to poison him with a blast of venomous herbs, instead of doing the Father harm, he himself dropped down in his sight." Among the evidences of deficient geographical knowledge in Gemelli's travels is a long discussion as to whether California is an island or part of the continent. The belief of a land connection between America and Asia was based on the story of a Christian slave at Peking who said that she had been brought from Mexico to China by way of Great Tartary. Russia and China were still far apart, though not entirely out of communication with one another. Gemelli gives an interesting account of a quarrel between the Chinese and Russians, or Muscovites as he calls them, about the pearl fishery of Lake Nepehyu, and how peace was restored by the good offices of some Jesuit missionaries. The result of the treaty was the arrival at Peking of "the ambassadors from the Great Duke of Muscovy, whom the Emperor received sitting on a throne raised twenty steps above the ground, whither he afterwards made them ascend to drink; and though they at first refused to touch the ground with their heads according to the custom of the country, at last they consented. They much admired to find a Tartar family in such majesty."

An Anglo-Indian Man of Letters.

In the beginning of the present year (1892) Anglo-Indian literature sustained a severe loss in the death of one who will always hold a high rank among its most accomplished journalists and men of letters. We refer to Mr. Curwen, the fatal termination of whose illness was marked by the suddenness that is such a terribly common feature in our life in this country. There was a consultation of doctors, a hurried embarkation of the sick man in the P. & O. steamer, and then, in six days, there came a telegram from Aden, conveying to his friends the sad intelligence that he had died in the Indian Ocean, only two days after his departure from Bombay.

There can be no doubt that Mr. Curwen's days were shortened by hard work and by the late hours that have to be kept by a journalist. No profession is more trying to health in this country than the press. To sit up late writing leading articles on the latest telegraphic intelligence is an unhealthy occupation anywhere, and, in the tropics, it is simply deadly.

Mr. Curwen came out to join the staff of the *Times of India* in 1877, and for fifteen years, first as assistant editor and afterwards as editor, gave himself up energetically to the work of the paper, and spared neither time, nor trouble, nor health in promoting its success. As a journalist he was distinguished by shrewd common sense, and by a quickness of insight which enabled him to take a clear view of a new situation of affairs with remarkable rapidity. If his articles did not actually lead public opinion, at any rate they were always well up to date, and thoroughly expressed the views of the Anglo-Indian community whom the *Times of India* represented. But we do not wish here to dwell upon this phase of his career. In spite of his marked success as a journalist, we cannot help regretting that Mr. Curwen lavished on the dry leading columns of a daily paper so much of the literary energy that might have been devoted to more congenial subjects. In his heart he took much more interest in *belles lettres* than in municipal disputes and the political questions of the day. Traces of this leaning might clearly be discerned in the conduct of the *Times of India* during all the years in which it was under his guidance. A large space was devoted to the review of literary works; on Saturday the leading columns were almost always open to the discussion of literary questions, or to the examination of some new book more or less connected with India; and there was also to be found in the body of the paper a large amount of original literary work.

It may be added that Mr. Curwen was always extremely ready to detect and encourage any evidence of literary talent, especially among young contributors. He took a kindly interest in every one who aspired, in however humble a way, to the honours of authorship, and was quick to discern the least sign of promise in their productions One of the last acts of his life was to bring out an edition of *Carlyle's Lectures on Literature,* the manuscript of which had long lain concealed from the world in the library of the Bombay Branch of the Asiatic Society. There was little or no chance of the speculation paying from a financial point of view. Yet the book was brought out regardless of expense, because it was not only a work of great literary interest, but was also likely to bring into notice a promising young Parsee writer, who, till then, had had no opportunity of distinguishing himself before the world. In many another case Mr. Curwen gave a helping hand to those who needed it. He did not confine his aid and sympathy to promising young writers, but was always ready to assist with his advice, as well as with his purse, those who had tried their hand at journalism unsuccessfully and fallen into destitution. To the subordinate members of his office he was a kind and liberal master, always generous to them in any difficulty, and willing to give them the much-needed rest that he too often denied himself.

Mr. Curwen had already gained some reputation as a writer in London before he left England. In the end of the year 1873, he brought out his *History of Booksellers*, a large work of five hundred pages, in which he sketched the rise and progress of the great English and Scotch publishing houses, and narrated the principal incidents in the lives of their founders. The book is full of lively anecdote and interesting information ; but, being of the nature of a compilation, it afforded the author little power of displaying his literary talents to advantage. A year later appeared *Sorrow and Song: Studies of Literary Struggle*, containing short biographies of Henry Murger, Novalis, Alexander Petöfi, Honoré de Balzac, Edgar Allan Poe, and André Chénier. This must have been a much more congenial task for its author than its predecessor. Himself a new writer, struggling for name and fame, he naturally had more sympathy for men of genius who had had a hard and painful struggle with adversity, than for prosperous booksellers. The lives are told with the enthusiasm which shows that the biographer loved his heroes in spite of their follies and their vices. In fact there is no doubt that, in the questions at issue between Philistia and Bohemia, Mr. Curwen was distinctly on the side of the Bohemian. His partiality for that mysterious and fascinating country is revealed again in the last work he brought out before he left England. This was a work of fiction called *Within Bohemia: or Love in London.* It came out in 1876, and was so successful, that a second edition was required in the following year. The review of the stories given in the *Academy*, remarks, that "the general effect of the volume is that of immaturity. Mr. Curwen's cleverness is quite undeniable, and, with all its faults of taste his book has more character and style than the ordinary novel." It was, as far as we know, his first attempt at fiction, and did not do more than give promise of the more excellent work, in the same line, that was to proceed from his pen at a later period, when his talents were matured by practice and a wider experience of the world and its inhabitants. Mr. Curwen would seem himself to have recognised the justice of the verdict of the *Academy* critic, for the heroine of one of his later and more mature works remarks, that "no man should ever be allowed to write a novel before he is forty," and, at the time of the publication of his Bohemian tales, he had not yet reached his thirtieth year.

For many years after his arrival in India, Mr. Curwen contributed nothing to general literature. His intellectual energy seemed to be entirely absorbed in his journalistic work. But all the while, in spite of incessant hard work and the imperious necessity of providing his leading columns daily with criticisms on current events, he must have been secretly cherishing an ideal life of imagination. For, in 1886, there appeared from his pen, in *Blackwood's Magazine*, the wonderful story of the early experiences of *Zit and Xoe*, a work full of poetic fancies and delicate humour, such as could hardly have been expected from a hard-worked Indian editor who had to spend most of his time in the Philistine labour of exchanging hard blows with his local contemporaries. Perhaps it was owing to a consciousness of this contrast, that this story in the magazine, and in its subsequent book form, and the two later works of fiction from the same pen, were published anonymously. The author may have thought that the production of such flowers of fancy might seem to the general public to be incompatible with his reputation as a newspaper editor holding practical views on the questions of the day. It is such a work as might naturally be attributed to a man of letters, who had retired, like Mr. Stevenson, from the hurry and skurry of civilised life, to the seclusion of some flowery isle in the sunny Pacific. For it is a tale of the days when the world was young, and when man and woman first began to look with joy and wonder on the beautiful world in which their lot was cast.

The idea of writing the story of Adam and Eve from a Darwinian point of view, is surely one of the happiest thoughts that ever entered the mind of an author in search of an original subject for a story. It is admirably worked out, and the result is an extremely beautiful prose idyll of love and family life. Mr. Curwen was neither a philosopher, nor a man of science. He makes no attempt to give a strictly realistic account of the life led by man before his intellect and moral sense were developed. If he had tried to do so, his work might have been interesting and instructive from a scientific point of view, but would have failed to give delight to the general reader. For the most part only such facts of early human existence as harmonise with a life that is not only simple but also beautiful, are introduced into the story. Thus we are given accounts of the invention of fish-hooks, of flint weapons, of fire, of pottery, and of boats, but all the more repulsive and ugly circumstances that must have attended the life of primitive man, are kept artistically in the background. In the characters of the hero and heroine, still less attempt is made at scientific accuracy. Their thoughts and emotions are such as could not possibly have belonged to beings immediately sprung from quadrumanous parents. Imagine the children of highly civilised parents, by some impossible means, to have survived and grown up to manhood and womanhood in the solitude of a beautiful desert island, and the result would be something like the delightful combination of primitive simplicity with half conscious instincts of the artificial conventions of polite society that is to be found in the characters of Zit and Xoe.

We all remember Eve's account of her first meeting with Adam in *Paradise Lost.* In Mr. Curwen's story it is Zit who relates the corresponding incident. By the shore of the sea, one day, a beautiful apparition came rushing towards him, as if borne on the wings of the wind. He pours forth compliments with a fervour and straightforwardness worthy of the first love of the first man who ever loved:—

"How beautiful you are! Your eyes are pure and blue. Your lips, when you smile, as you did for a little while at first, are far redder than the sweetest roses. I never saw anything like the way your colour comes and goes. And why are you so fair, and why is your hair so long and golden, and why are your hands so white and tiny?" And, quite unconsciously, I tried to take one of her hands in mine.

She drew herself up, and her blue eyes had a strange reproachful look. "I am certain," she said very slowly, "that it is not right of you to speak like that. And you really talk so quickly, that I cannot follow half of what you say."

"You would talk quickly, too," I retorted, "if you were talking for the first time in your life." . . .

I had been watching her eyes and her lips so eagerly, that I had never noticed that she was sitting all this time upon the back of a beautiful white horse, and that she was robed, almost from head to foot, in some soft, whitey-yellowy fleecy stuff. Both her round arms were bare, and one shoulder quite free. She had a broad girdle of plaited golden grass about her waist, and bunches of great yellow lilies on her breast and in her hair. I always think of Xoe as I saw her then: lithesome, free, and beautiful, in this flowing, clinging garment, with one little hand caressing and restraining her fiery steed, with her drooping eyes and faint smile and fleeting blushes.

A beautiful subject for a painting or a sculpture, bright and graceful as the Europa of Moschus borne by the divine bull over the waves of the Bosphorus with her purple robes flowing in the breeze! The mysterious robe in which Xoe was clad was made of the great cocoons of tussar silk that she had noticed clinging to the mulberry trees. She had watched the spiders for days working at their webs, and had learnt from them how to spin. Zit thought he also must go in for clothes, but he made them so rudely of deerskins that, to his great chagrin, the fair Xoe only laughed at him for his pains:—

"That is really nice of you," she said, trying to stop laughing, "and it suits you exactly. Please, don't think me rude. I can't help it"—and here she fairly broke down—"but it does so remind me of the fright I made of myself two days after I ran away. I wonder if you went down to the river, too, and looked into it, and how long you stopped there?"

My conscience pricked me here, and I cried out rather bitterly—"You are really too bad, Xoe!"

Her voice changed at once. "I am not bad," she answered. "I don't know how to explain it, but a girl never says what she thinks. If you want to get on with me, you must not believe a word I say, and when I cry and laugh, you must not believe me either. There! It is horrible, but ever since yesterday morning, I have felt it to be true. I don't know why I should warn you like this—perhaps, because I feel it is good of you and kind of you to take such a world of trouble to do what you think I wish, and really you would not look nice in tussar silk."

This mollified me, of course, and as we sat over breakfast, I said, "I hope you did not think I had gone for ever, Xoe; I was afraid you would be frightened."

"Oh dear, no!" she replied with half a pout: "I saw your stick directly I came out. I knew you would never leave that; and then—I was here too."

In the above passage we have a good specimen of the art with which Mr. Curwen works into his story, not too obtrusively, reminiscences of *Paradise Lost.* It will be remembered how, soon after her creation, Eve lay down to look into the clear, smooth lake that seemed another sky :—

> " As I bent down to look, just opposite
> A shape within the watery gleam appeared,
> Bending to look on me ; I started back,
> It started back ; but, pleased, I soon return'd ;
> Pleased, it returned as soon with answering looks
> Of sympathy and love.

Xoe, and seemingly Zit, too, were guilty of the same weakness as Milton's Eve. The stick, so archly referred to by Xoe, was a walking-stick which Zit had carved for himself in his lonely days, and which had been his only companion until he met Xoe.

We have not space to dwell longer on the courtship of Zit and Xoe, or to tell how Xoe's cruelty and perverseness drove him to encounter a big black bear with an aggravating sardonic grin, by which he would have been killed, had not Xoe come in the nick of time and saved his life. He recovered from his swoon to find himself lying with his head on her lap, and the big black bear lying stone dead beside them.

"Who killed him?" I asked, still bewildered, trying to rise to my feet.

"Be quiet, Zit!" said Xoe very softly. "I killed him, dear. I could not help it. I thought he had killed you. Don't be cross to me now. I will never be cross to you again."

"Poor thing," she went on, "how pale you looked! I saw nothing but you, and I pushed your big spear right through that horrible beast. He fell away, and I have been sitting here with your head in my lap ever since. What a dreadful world it is! and all, I know, on my account. But I could not help it, and I can't help it, Zit. Do say that I was right and that I could not help it."

The author shows much artistic skill in tracing the gradual transformation by which the waywardness and liveliness of Xoe's "uncertain, coy, and hard to please" maidenhood was converted into the mellower grace of a wife and a mother. Suffice it to say that she remains equally charming to the end, even to the last scene of all, when, as a great-great-grandmother, she looks over her husband's shoulder, and gives his white hair the loving little pat that always presages a scolding. Enough has surely been quoted to show what a pleasure is in store for those who have not yet read this delightful prose idyll. Yet the story is not one that gains by the process of selection, as it is an admirably finished piece of literary work from beginning to end, full of delicate humour, lively dialogue, and beautiful descriptions of natural scenery.

The scene of Mr. Curwen's next book opens in the garden of Eden; not in the luxuriant tropical scenery where Zit and Xoe loved each other in the morning of the world, but in the veritable Garden of Eden as it exists in the present day: "a dank, desolate marsh, where the muddy waters of the Tigris and the Euphrates meet together." Here Mr. Hicks, the hero, into whose mouth is put the story of *Lady Bluebeard*, met his Eve in the person of Mrs. Fonblanque. She coolly sat down on the trunk of the Tree of Good and Evil, which he had just had cut down for the benefit of an uncle who loved such interesting curios. Mrs. Fonblanque and Xoe are about as unlike each other as two women who are both very charming could possibly be. This difference might naturally be expected between two persons separated by all the centuries that have rolled away since the time when man first appeared on the earth. The heroine of *Lady Bluebeard* is a typical woman of the nineteenth century, the result of many centuries of evolution and culture. Although she is always witty and often light-hearted, her life has been saddened for ever by an unfortunate early marriage, and her modern education and refinement have spread the "pale cast of thought" over her brow. She is past the first joyousness of youth; her experience of life, so far, has been very melancholy; and when she meets her new lover she is wandering rather aimlessly about the world, in the vain attempt to escape from bitter memories. Yet, like many a lady in real life who has gone through a discipline of sorrow, she is very charming, and does much to make those around her happy by her vivacity, her unselfishness, and her gentle sympathy. Her character is beautifully drawn, and has the strong individuality that cannot be given to a fictitious personage, unless its creator has a touch of genius. The love story contained in the novel is so very bare of incidents, that it would hardly afford sufficient material for a short story in *Belgravia* or *Temple Bar.* It must also be allowed that the few incidents of which the plot is composed, are extremely unnatural, and that the conclusion is melodramatic. Nevertheless, in this long-drawn narrative, the character of the hero, and still more that of the heroine, are made to unfold themselves clearly to the reader with so much artistic skill that he is entirely

E

fascinated with the book from beginning to end, and, in spite of the absence of exciting incidents, the interest never flags.

This fascination is partly due to the psychological insight of the author, and partly to the fact, that *Lady Bluebeard* contains elements of interest not to be found in ordinary novels. The leading characters reveal themselves, not so much by what they do, as by what they say. They have long discussions on all kinds of interesting questions, such as the position of women, poetry, painting, heredity, and pessimism. There are also three chapters of clever satire which describe England as seen through Oriental spectacles, after the manner of Goldsmith's *Citizen of the World*. These discussions, besides familiarising us with the speakers, have an interest of their own. Owing to the wit of the dialogue and the suggestiveness and variety of the thoughts expressed, *Lady Bluebeard* may be compared with such works as *The Autocrat of the Breakfast Table*, *Guesses at Truth* and Landor's *Imaginary Conversations*, and does not suffer from the comparison. There is yet a third distinct point of interest in *Lady Bluebeard*, inasmuch as the book is a record of the personal observations made by the author in his holiday tours. The greater portion of the two volumes gives a faithful description of what is to be seen in a voyage from Baghdad to Bombay. We have known travellers by this route who have taken *Lady Bluebeard* with them and found it a most admirable guide-book. This might, at first blush, seem to be a disparaging remark, did we not remember that Scott's *Lady of the Lake* has been, for nearly a century, a necessary part of the equipment of Highland tourists.

Mr. Curwen's descriptions of Oriental scenery, and of the cities of Asia and their inhabitants, are wonderfully animated and picturesque. Here, for instance, is an admirable sketch of an Arabian town, struck off in a few bold strokes :—

"But now turn your chair quickly round, Mr. Hicks. What do you think of that for the Gulf ?"

I am seldom profoundly impressed, but I had certainly never seen anything like this. We were steaming rapidly, as I turned, right into a huge wall of precipitous volcanic rocks. Suddenly we rounded the point, and glided smoothly into a quiet little cove, surrounded on its three sides by towering black hills and rugged mountains. The nearest hills and crags and peaks to the right and left, looking each one of them like an iron-bound fortress, dropped sheer and bluff to the water's edge. At either extremity a strong fortress scowled fiercely down upon us, and a number of smaller forts and watch-towers and galleries seemed to connect the two in a semi-circle behind. The shore was low and open for a little way in front, and there, between the black rocks and the blue sea, nestled a town of white flat-roofed houses.

We anchored within a cable's length of the Sultan's palace, with his blood-red flag still streaming over it. There was not a tree or shrub to be seen. But the white houses, the turreted forts, the deep blue sea, and the quaint craft with which the little cove was half filled, contrasted strangely with the encircling masses of dark rock all around, and a sky that was, for a moment before the sun sank, flooded with gold and crimson. To enjoy the first view of Muscat properly, you should come straight upon it, as we did, from a tedious sea voyage along the arid coast of Persia, and you should enter the harbour exactly as the sun is going down. In another moment the sunset guns were thundering and reverberating among the rocks, and then all was still, except when a deep voice from a mosque-tower, here and there, summoned the Faithful to prayers.

The same pen that traced the stern outlines of

the picture given above, was equally, or, if possible, even more felicitous in painting the rich and various colours of the forests of Ceylon, of Indian architecture, and of the motley crowds who kept holiday at Baroda on the occasion of the Gaekwar's wedding. Indeed, it is impossible to read *Lady Bluebeard* without being convinced that Mr. Curwen, if he had chosen to travel through Asia and give an account of his journey, might have rivalled the author of *Eothen.*

Mr. Curwen's last work was *Dr. Hermione*, published in 1890. It is less closely connected with India than his two previous works of fiction. In *Zit and Xoe*, although, consistently with the chronology of the story, no geographical names are introduced, the beautiful pictures of tropical scenery are evidently drawn from the author's experience of India. The heroine of *Lady Bluebeard* is an Anglo-Indian lady, and the narrative conducts us by way of the Persian Gulf to Bombay, and subsequently to Baroda, Goa, and Ceylon. In *Dr. Hermione*, although the two heroes of the story are officers of the Indian army, the scene of the story is laid first in Cumberland and then in Egypt. Mr. Curwen was a native of the English Lake Country, in which his family had been settled for many generations. In the beginning of

Dr. Hermione, he returns to the scenes of his youth, and paints the lights and shadows of the mountain scenery of the lakes with loving fidelity. Towards the end of the novel, the scene is abruptly changed to the southern borders of Egypt, where, after a skirmish with the Dervishes, the characters pair off with one another to their own satisfaction and that of the reader. We can pardon the abruptness of the transition, in consideration of the beautiful descriptions of the banks of the Nile which it enables the author to give us. Here, too, as in *Lady Bluebeard,* our author is drawing upon his own experiences as a traveller. Some time before he wrote *Dr. Hermione* he had taken a holiday trip up the Nile; and the glowing account of the beauties of that famous river is a record of what he then observed. As a story, *Dr. Hermione* is characterised by the same want of incident that distinguishes *Lady Bluebeard* from most novels; and here, again, the paucity of incident is almost forgotten, owing to the brightness of the dialogue and the descriptive power of the writer. So much is said and so little is done, that the work has more of the nature of a drama than of a novel. The characters of the chief persons are revealed, as in *Lady Bluebeard,* by their conversations much more than by their actions. They are all interesting sketches, although none of them can be considered such a highly finished portrait as Mrs. Fonblanque.

In looking back on Mr. Curwen's three works of fiction, we find that they are weakest in their plots. The author does not appear to have cared much for probability or consistency in the construction of his narrative. In *Zit and Xoe,* the subject chosen was such a happy one, that a very simple succession of incidents was sufficient to supply the thread of the story. In *Lady Bluebeard* and *Dr. Hermione* there is little action, and the few incidents that are related do not seem to be very naturally connected with each other. Even in minor details little attention is paid to minute accuracy. In the description of a boat adventure in *Dr. Hermione,* the wind seems to be blowing in two opposite directions; but that perhaps may be defended, on Virgil's precedent, as a characteristic of fictitious storms On one occasion, when the sea was spread before Zit's eyes "in almost unruffled beauty," he nevertheless relates how "laughing and splashing and sparkling just beneath my feet, its white spray glistened like rainbows." Such inconsistencies, however, are but small matters. The greatest of all novelists, in an elaborate description of a storm, made the sun set in the east. Such trifling slips, though interesting to the curious critic, have little weight with us when we try to estimate the general merits of a work of fiction.

Mr. Curwen's literary work ought, moreover, to be judged from a different point of view. He was, in reality, more of a humorist than of a novelist, although he happened to express his humour in the form of fiction. When we call him a humorist, we do not use the term as applied in America to such writers as Bill Nye and Artemus Ward, but in the wider and nobler sense in which the term is used by Thackeray. To be a humorist, in this higher sense of the word, requires high intellectual gifts, and keen insight into human character. In this latter qualification, Mr. Curwen excelled, especially in knowledge of the weakness and strength of female character. Xoe, Mrs. Fonblanque, Edith, and Dr. Hermione are real women, very unlike each other, and are all very interesting psychological studies. There is less individuality to be found among Mr. Curwen's men. Mr. Hicks, travelling over the world in search of intellectual excitement, is a modernised repetition of Zit wandering through the primeval forests in which he found "so much to see and so much to taste." Dr. Jones, with his shrewdness and his kindly nature concealed under a transparent veil of cynicism, is probably what Mr. Hicks would have developed into, if circumstances had confined him, until advanced middle age, in a remote provincial town. Nevertheless, Zit, Mr. Hicks, and Dr. Jones, in spite of the family likeness that exists between them, are full of life and very real, and admirably adapted to play their respective parts as contrasts to the female characters to whom the author devotes most of his attention.

In the portrayal of the various male and female characters whom he creates, Mr. Curwen shows a delicate sense of humour, and a knowledge of human character, that amply atone for any deficiencies in the plots of the stories. His novels, too, are as much distinguished by wit as by humour. They are, as we have seen, full of long conversations which would be wearisome to the reader, if they were not lightened up by epigram, satire, and acute criticism of literature, art, men, and manners.

As a writer of English prose, Mr. Curwen appears at his best in descriptive passages. His style is admirable in its clearness and freedom from all mannerism and affectation. In his pages we find the lonely forests and the populous cities of the East described with equal vividness, so that the whole scene is conjured up before the imagination of the reader with the perfect art by which art is concealed. The simplicity and unstudied grace of his style is very unlike the artificial brilliancy of that of Sterne, whom he resembles in his subtle and rather whimsical humour; in the skill with which he makes the most ordinary situations amusing or pathetic, or both; in his fondness for digressions; in his tendency to relate actual experiences of travel in a fictitious setting, and, finally, in the poverty of incident and the very subordinate position of the story in his literary works. But for this difference, we should be almost inclined to regard Mr. Curwen as a nineteenth century Anglo-Indian Sterne.

In spite of the chorus of recognition with which the reviewers greeted the appearance of his later works, we hardly think that Mr. Curwen has yet met with the appreciation due to his very great literary merits. This is, no doubt, partly due to the fact that his latest and best works were produced anonymously. It is only under very exceptional circumstances that the general public does justice to an anonymous writer. Further, Mr. Curwen devoted to his journalistic profession a large amount of the intellectual energy which he might have bestowed on literary work of a higher character, and, just when, in spite of these drawbacks, he was establishing for himself a high position in the literary world, his career was suddenly cut short. As it is, however, he has left behind him, in *Zit and Xoe* and *Lady Bluebeard*, two works of great originality that will not soon be allowed to be forgotten, and, in the rather barren roll of Anglo-Indian literature, he must assuredly take the very highest rank among those who have succeeded in throwing the glamour of romance and poetry over life in the East.

before he was establishing for himself a high position in the literary world—his career was suddenly cut short. As it is, however, he has left behind him in *Edward Roy* and *Lady Blanchard*, two works of great originality that will not soon be allowed to be forgotten, and in the rather barren field of Anglo-Indian literature he must assuredly take the very highest rank among those who have succeeded in throwing the glamour of romance and poetry over life in the East.

Anglo-Indian Words and Phrases.

From a philological point of view India is now in a position similar to that of England immediately after the Norman Conquest, and to her own former position at the period of her history when Mahomedan invaders introduced Persian and Arabic into the country. Just as in England, after the Norman Conquest, there were two nations living side by side, speaking different languages, and striving to render themselves comprehensible to each other, so now in India we find everywhere Englishmen speaking English, and the natives of the country speaking their vernacular, and, as intermediaries between the two, the educated native and the Englishman who has mastered Hindustani, Marathi, Gujarathi, or whatever vernacular is spoken in the part of the country in which he dwells. Norman-French and Anglo-Saxon, after one or two centuries, coalesced into one language, and in like manner the mixture of Persian and Arabic with Indian vernaculars produced Hindustani. We have, at the present time, the first steps of a similar fusion between the English language and the vernaculars of India, a process which, if continued for a century or two, would produce a new composite language, partly of Eastern and partly of European origin. At present, however, we are only at the very beginning of such a fusion. English and the vernaculars are still separated from each other by a great gulf. Nevertheless, they cannot be in such close contact without a large amount of mutual action and re-action, which will be found, on consideration, to be regulated by the same laws as ruled the early relations of English with Norman French at the Conquest, and subsequently with the other foreign languages spoken by the nations with which the enterprising spirit of Englishmen has brought them into commercial and political intercourse all over the world.

The philological results of the British Empire in India may be briefly summed up as follows: firstly, that many Indian words have been introduced into the English language; secondly, that many English words have been introduced into the vernaculars of India; and thirdly, that several English words and several Indian words have assumed new senses and new combinations, owing to the social intercourse between Englishmen and natives of India.

Let us first consider the words of Indian origin

that have been added to the English language. Some of them are of such old standing that they are thoroughly naturalised. The most rigid purist might use such words as "punkah," "Brahmin," "pariah," "curry," "jungle," "rajah," and "rupee." They need not be printed in italics in English books, and are given a place even in small English dictionaries. Among these words that have been admitted into full English citizenship, may, perhaps, be counted "salam," one of the most interesting words that India has given to England. The earliest use of this greeting by an European writer quoted in Yule and Burnell's *Hobson Jobson*, is a passage from Correa, a Portuguese writer who visited India in the year 1512. But the European use of the word goes back to a much earlier date than the sixteenth century. Some time ago, in turning over the pages of Symonds' *Greek Poets*, I came upon an epitaph written on himself by Meleager, a Greek epigrammatist, who flourished at Gadara, the town so familiar to us as the home of the Gadarene swine, just before the Christian era. It gave me a shock of surprise to find in this epigram the familiar word "salam" in Greek letters. The epitaph ends by addressing the supposed visitor to his tomb as follows: "If you are a Syrian, Salam; if you are a Phœnician, Naidios;

and if a Greek, Chaire."[1] These lines show that "salam" was the ordinary word of salutation throughout Syria at the beginning of the Christian era. We might, therefore, conjecture that "salam" was one of the words most frequently in the mouth of Christ and his Apostles. This conjecture is raised almost to a certainty by reference to the Gospels. "Salam" is an Arabic word, meaning peace; and Christ, in taking farewell of his Apostles, says, "Peace I leave with you; my peace I give unto you: not as the world giveth, give I unto you." There is little doubt that the very word on that occasion actually used by Christ and translated *eirene*, peace, was "salam." The meaning of the text is that Christ did not leave his disciples an ordinary, meaningless, verbal salam, but the priceless thing which "salam" really means, namely peace. We may, therefore, without hesitation add "salam" to the small list of words which we know to have been really spoken by Christ.

While such words as salam, punkah, and jungle are sufficiently naturalised to be used by the most scrupulous English writer, there are many other Indian words that are struggling for their English citizenship, and are mostly found in conversation,

[1] 'Αλλ' ἐι μέν Σύρος ἐσσι, ΣΑΛΑΜ, εἰ δ' οὖν σύ γε Φόινιξ,
ΝΑΙ ΔΙΟΣ, εἰ δ "Ελλην, ΧΑΙΡΕ. τὸ δ' αὐτὸ φράσον.

as *loot, tappal, dubber, pucka, cutcha,* and others too many to mention. In some cases Indian words used by Englishmen change their meaning. Thus "toddy," which, in its Indian sense, means the juice of the palm tree, has come to mean in English the combination of spirits and hot water, that is so popular a remedy against the cold and mists of Scotland. A bazaar in English generally means a fancy fair, and not a market-place. The term "lascar," applied to Indian sailors, is derived from *lashkar*, an army. *Sidi*, a Hindustani word connected with the Arabic *saiyid*, a lord, was once a title of honour, and retains its old sense when applied to the Prince of Jingeera; but in Anglo-Indian usage, the poorest Africans who work at the docks, or in the engine rooms of steamers, are called Seedees, or Seedy boys. "Faujdar," from *fauj*, an army, properly means a general, but we apply the originally proud title to a chief policeman, even though he may be the chief policeman of a small town, with only some three or four men under his command. *Mashal*, a lamp or torch in Hindustani, means, in Bombay, the servant who looks after the lamps, undergoing a change of meaning by metonymy similar to that by which, in ordinary English, "spears," "oars," and "rifles" can stand for "spearmen," "oarsmen," and "riflemen."

In some cases the Indian word changes its grammatical character when adopted into English. The noun *jawab*, an answer, does duty as an Anglo-Indian verb, when we talk of a suitor being *jawaubed*, that is, refused. *Khaki* is properly an adjective meaning "of the colour of dust." As used in English, it is a noun, meaning cloth of that colour. *Jaldi*, an adverb meaning "quickly," is converted into a noun by the British soldier when he calls upon dawdling natives to "put a little more *jaldi* into it." The imperatives of several common Indian verbs are, in Anglo-Indian conversation, treated as the stems of verbs, and have the ordinary English verbal inflections added to them. One such strangely-formed verb has been thoroughly naturalised in English. "Shampoo" is, by origin, the imperative of the Hindustani verb *champna*, but in English it entirely loses its imperative force, and is conjugated as a verb of the weak conjugation, with "shampooed" as its past tense and past participle. *Puckerao*, *samjhao maro*, and *banao* are likewise colloquially conjugated as English verbs, especially by English soldiers. *Banao* is not only used as a verbal stem but also as a noun. When Bellew's Griffin buys a pariah dog, docked and cropped to make him look like a terrier, his more experienced friend asks him, "Where on earth did you get this beast? Why, he's a regular terrier bunnow." In ordinary English we can find instances of imperatives thus used as nouns, as when a child says, "It is all make-believe," or a parliamentary reporter talks of a "count-out." A similar change of grammatical value, not unlike that undergone by the Hindustani imperatives converted into Anglo-Indian verbal stems, occurred when such verbs as "complicate" and "affect" were formed out of Latin passive participles. But I cannot remember any instance, except those just mentioned, of imperatives of foreign verbs being used as new English verbs. How it happened, is clear enough. The words that we have been considering were continually used in the imperative mood, as words of command, by Englishmen to their servants and others, and became so familiar that the imperative inflection was regarded as an essential part of the verb. If the records of history were destroyed, and these verbs, formed from Indian imperatives, still survived, they would give clear evidence of the ruling position held by the English in India, just as the consideration of the French word "mutton," side by side with the Anglo-Saxon word "sheep," indicates that long ago the Saxon shepherds herded sheep which did not become familiar to their Norman masters until the animal appeared in a cooked form on the table, as mutton.

Having seen that the Englishman makes new verbs out of the imperatives of Indian verbs, and out of the passive participles of Latin verbs, we may finish what is to be said on the subject of the naturalisation of foreign verbs, by inquiring, how the native of India is inclined to treat the English verbs he uses. As a rule, we shall find that our native servants and other uneducated natives, who have a smattering of English, confine themselves to the use of the present participle to express all moods and tenses. We find this predominance of the present participle correctly illustrated by the remarks of the Moonshee in the *Lays of Ind.*:—

"He also said, Sáib pray excuse, but what will master do,—
What master giving Moonshee man, if master getting through?
Two hundred fifty rupee, sircar backsheesh, Sáib will get;
Sáibs always giving Moonshee half, got never less, Sir, yet.
I always coming reglar, teaching good."

From a consideration of this tendency, it seems probable that, if an English verb is ever naturalised in an Indian vernacular, it will be in the permanent form of a present participle. It is easy to see how uneducated natives should be inclined to fix upon one particular part of the English verb for constant use. To do so saves the trouble of mastering the inflexions and auxiliaries, by which, in English, moods and tenses are distinguished. The reason why the present participle is chosen in preference to any other part of the English verb, would seem to be the prevalence of the use of tenses formed from the present participle in Hindustani and other Indian vernaculars.

Of the Indian words used by Englishmen, several have gained acceptance from a resemblance to English words of similar meaning. The Englishman in India soon picks up the word *gari*, and fixes it in his memory, as he connects it in his mind with the English word carriage. In the same way *bat cheet* reminds him of chit chat, and *gup* looks like an abbreviation of "gossip." "Beastie" is a Scotch diminutive applied as a term of endearment to animals. Thus Burns addresses the mouse as a "wee, sleekit, cowrin', timorous beastie." The term is, perhaps, most commonly used by Scotch drovers, when speaking of their cattle. So, when we are told in India that the man who brings us water in puckals on an ox's back is a bheestie, it is easy to remember the name. We simply extend to the Indian combination of man and beast, the term that is applied to the beast alone by the Scotch Highlander.

In a very large number of cases the Indian word has been Anglicised by alteration in sound, or at any rate in spelling, so as to make it resemble English words and syllables. Such corruptions of unfamiliar foreign words into more familiar and intelligible sounds are common in every language. The French *contre danse*, meaning a dance in which the dancers stand face to face, was corrupted in England into "country dance," and *chartreux* and *chateau vert* become, in English, Charterhouse and Shotover. The old alliance between France and Scotland has given the Scotch language "petticoat tails," which is a pretty corruption of the French *petits gatedux.* In like manner the English sailor converts the Bellerophon and the Pteroessa into the Billy Ruffian and Tearing Hisser. This tendency can be largely illustrated by Anglo-Indian instances. In some cases the corruption merely secures a familiar sound, without regard to meaning. Take, for instance, the word punch, derived from *panch*, five, because the beverage is composed of five ingredients, namely, spirits, lime juice, sugar, spice, and water. "Punch," in more senses than one, is a familiar monosyllable in "English"; but no ingenuity can naturally connect any of its meanings with the drink which, in its cold form, proved so seductive to Mr. Pickwick. There is a similar disregard of meaning in the corruption of *kabáb, tám-tám, Nawáb, báp-re, pandi-kokku* into "cabob," "tom-tom," "nawab," "bobbery," and "bandi-coot." In these cases the familiar English syllables "tom," "bob" and "coot" are got into the word by hook or by crook, without any regard to the sense. In most cases, however, there is enough connection between the corruption and its meaning to suggest, more or less distinctly, a false etymology. Sometimes the association of ideas is very slight. "Jolly boat" appears to be derived from the Indian *gallevat;* but the most etymological sailor would scarcely maintain that such a boat is any jollier than a cutter or a dingy, which two terms, by-the-bye, are also traced by Yule to an Indian origin. It was scarcely from any recognition of chivalric traits in his character that Clive's soldiers dubbed Surajah Dowlah a knight under the title of Sir Roger Dowlah. When *malli* was corrupted into "molly," there was, perhaps, underlying the transformation, the thought that the name given to the English housemaid might, without impropriety, be transferred to the not very manly Indian gardener.

In other cases, however, the connection in meaning is too obvious to be denied. Perhaps the most striking Anglo-Indian instance of this tendency to find a false etymology is the verb "dumb cow," one of those Anglo-Indian verbs formed from Indian imperatives. It comes from *dam khao*, the imperative of the Hindustani *dam khana*, to eat one's breath, that is, to be silent. The Anglo-Indian derivative is spelt "dumbcow," so as to give both syllables an English meaning, and raise in the mind the idea of cowing a person and rendering him dumb, or of making him as dumb as a cow. *Sitaphal*, the fruit of Sita, one of the Indian names of what we usually call the custard apple, is ingeniously corrupted into "sweet apple." "Breach Candy," the name of a favourite drive by the sea in Bombay, is derived by Dr. Murray Mitchell from *Burj-Khádi*, the tower of the creek. If this is the correct derivation, the word has been corrupted into "Breach Candy" in order to make it intelligible to English ears, for "breach," connected with "break," in old and provincial English means an inlet of the sea, for instance in *Judges* v. 17, where we read, that "Asher continued on the sea-shore and abode in his breaches." Such an inlet is marked as "The Breach" on an old map of Bombay, at one end of what is now Breach Candy. The Apollo Bunder, at which the P. and O. steamers land their Bombay passengers, seems to have been originally called after a fish which still appears occasionally on Western-Indian breakfast tables, the *palla* bunder, until the English settlers, more familiar with classical mythology than with Indian ichthyology, corrupted *palla* into Apollo. "Biscobra," from *biskhapra*, like "dumbcow," is so converted as to provide a double false etymology intelligible to an Englishman, and suggest that the mysterious lizard meant has twice the venom of the cobra. The Hindustani *idhar ao* is converted into *hitherao*, in order that it may contain the English adverb "hither." The Bengali *gudám*, a store-house, is converted into go-down. The derivation suggested by the change, though false, is plausible, as in the East store-houses are generally under ground, so that their owner has to *go down* into them. "Teapoy" is, by derivation, *tinpai*, a three-footed table, just as "charpoy" is a four-footed bed. But it is small and convenient for tea; and therefore the first syllable is spelt accordingly. In like manner, from the association of ideas shown above, "bheesty" is often spelt "beasty"; "Solar *tope*" is from *shola*, meaning pith, which is converted into the English adjective "solar," from Latin *sol*, the sun, in order that "solar tope" may convey to an Englishman's ear, by its sound and spelling, the appropriate meaning of sun helmet. "Hanger" is generally supposed to be derived from the verb "hang," because a sword hangs by one's side. It is really the same word as the Scotch "whinger," and is derived from the Arabic and Hindustani *khangar*.

Yule quotes an instance of the use of the word as early as 1574, so that it probably came from Arabia at the time of the Crusades, rather than, at a later date, from India. As the word was more common in Scotland than in England, it may have been brought back by the survivors of the 15,000 Highlanders and Islesmen who, according to William of Malmesbury, went to Palestine in the eleventh century. The abbreviation of *chithi* and *tattoo* into the Anglo-Indian "chit" and "tat" may also be, perhaps, regarded as the result of etymological corruption. The associations of the English word "chit," generally meaning a small girl, seem to have affected the Anglo-Indian word, so that "chit" in our colloquial language is used rather of a small note sent by messenger, than of a regular full-sized letter. *Tattoo,* by being abbreviated into "tat," suggests to the English mind the old English word "tit," meaning a small horse or pony. "Gymkhana," about the derivation of which there has been so much discussion and doubt, is almost certainly an instance of etymological corruption. Unless the word is a hybrid, which is unlikely, its first syllable is a corruption of some Indian word. But of what word? Whitworth makes no conjecture on the subject. Yule says that "gymkhana" is probably a corruption of *gend khana,* ball house, the name generally given to a racket court. Is it not, however, more probable that the origin of the word is *jamatkhana*, a place of assembly, a word familiar enough to be given in Whitworth's Anglo-Indian dictionary? Is not this the word that would most naturally be used by natives to express the central place of the station, where the *Sahib logue* meet to enjoy themselves after the labours of the day? That the idea of meeting is the idea most naturally connected with "gymkhana" is indicated by Yule himself, who, though he gives a different derivation, describes a gymkhana as "a place of public resort at a station." *Jam*, the beginning of the word, would easily and naturally be corrupted into "gym" in English conversation, as the gymkhana is a place of active exercise, and so has some resemblance to a gymnasium. There is less uncertainty about the etymology of a strange corruption of Indian words by which the English soldier at Satara found what he thought a suitable name for the game of badminton. When that game was first introduced at Satara, the natives called it *tam-tam-phul-khel* (the tom-tom flower game), because the battledoor with which it was originally played resembled a tom-tom, and the shuttle-cock looked like a flower. The British soldier, hearing this name, and determined to give it an intelligible meaning, transformed it into Tom Fool Game, by which means he both satisfied his etymological instincts, and also contrived to express his very decided opinion of the frivolity of the new game.

We may now leave words of purely Indian origin and proceed to consider those which are partly of English and partly of Indian origin. There are a certain number of words that we use in India, each of which appears, on consideration, to be the result of the blending into one of two words resembling each other in sound and in meaning, but belonging to different languages. For instance, when we are making a bargain with a native carpenter, or tailor, he will promise to do his work *praper*. Who can decide whether this is a corruption of the Indian *barabar*, to make it sound like the English "proper," or vice versâ? The truth seems to be that it is a compromise between the two similar sounds. Take again the term "boy," used in addressing native servants. How can it be determined whether this is the English "boy," a term which, like the modern French *garçon*, and the Latin *puer*, was commonly applied to grown-up servants in the seventeenth century, or the Indian *boi*, the name of a caste much employed in Madras as palanquin bearers and domestic servants. A similar double origin is required to explain "bearer," which is to a large extent the Bengal equivalent of the term "boy," as used in Madras and Bombay. *Behārā*, we learn from Whitworth, is, in Bengali, as *boi* is in Telugu, the name of a caste that supplies palkhiwalas and domestic servants. Thus, when in Bengal the Englishman called the men who carried his palkhi, his bearers, although he usually spelt the word as if it were formed from the English verb "bear," it is impossible to say that the word was more of English than of Indian origin. Afterwards the meaning of "bearer" in Bengal changed. From being applied to the palanquin bearers, it was transferred to the single servant of the same caste who took care of his master's clothes, and thus the word has attained its present meaning. Another case of double derivation is "wordie," an order, which seems to result from the fusion of the Kanarese *varadi*, an order, with the English noun "word," often employed in giving an order, as when we say, "send word to so-and-so to come quickly." It is strange, in Swift's *Polite Conversation*, to come upon the sentence: "O! miss, you must give your vardi too!" Very unsatisfactory explanations are given of "vardi" in this context. Some say it is for *par dieu;* some declare it to be an affected pronunciation of "verdict." May it not be that the term is the Indian word *varadi,* and that it was introduced into English polite conversation by some Anglo-Indian, who returned to England in the days of Swift? Such out-of-the-way words often gain a temporary vogue in fashionable conversation, and then disappear to give place to others. "Cot" and "buggy" are two other terms which can, with equal ease, be traced to Indian and English origin. But perhaps the most familiar instance of this confusion is the Anglo-Indian "tank," which differs slightly in meaning from the English word "tank," and slightly in form from the Indian word *tanka.* No doubt the Englishman or the Portuguese—for a word of the same sound and derivation, but of different spelling, is in the Portuguese language also,— on landing in India and hearing the word *tanka* applied to a reservoir of water, identified it immediately with the similar word in his own language, so that this Anglo-Indian word may perhaps be described as of threefold derivation.

Words and phrases of mixed origin are more easily treated when the parts derived from different languages are kept separate in different syllables. Ordinary English hybrids, such as "bigamy" and "tidology," may be paralleled by several similar Anglo-Indian combinations, as, for instance, brandy-pawnee, agboat, competitionwala, missee baba, memsahib, purdah lady, travellers' bungalow. In several of these hybrids we have additional instances of the tendency to corrupt unfamiliar into familiar sounds. Mr. Stanley Lane Poole says that "John Company" was originally Jahan-Kumpani (Company of the World), the name given by the natives of India to the United East India Company. The *kālij* pheasant of the Himalayas is rather absurdly converted into a college-pheasant, much as Uxford, the river ford (*cf.* Uxbridge), was changed into Oxford. Jack, in "Jack-fruit" is a corruption of the Malay *chakka*, or rather of the Portuguese word derived from the Malay. "First chop" was originally first *chāp*, or first stamp, *chāp* being the word we are familiar with in *chāpakhāna*, a printing house. According to Yule, "quite the cheese" is literally quite the thing, "cheese" being a corruption of the common Hindustani word *chiz*, a thing. He also traces the offending word in a phrase generally supposed to savour of blasphemy to an Indian origin, in *dām*, the name of a copper coin worth a fortieth part of a rupee. Certainly the etymological analogy of the kindred phrases, "don't care a curse" and "don't care a rap," support his view. For a rap was a small Irish coin, and "curse," in the phrase, "I don't care a curse," is undoubtedly a corruption of the harmless "kerse," which in Chaucer meant "cress."

The words which we have next to consider are those of English origin that have gained currency in vernacular writing or conversation, or have attained a new meaning in India. In so doing, it will be convenient to treat as of English origin all the words that have come to India from England, whatever may have been their ultimate origin. We must also, of course, regard Scotch as English. Indeed, the language of Burns has much more right to the name of English than is possessed by the literary English to which that name is generally confined; for Lowland Scotch, as is clearly shown by Earle, is the direct descendant of the language spoken in the Anglican kingdom of Northumbria, while literary English is descended from the language spoken by the Saxon kingdoms of Central and Southern England, and altered by the admixture of Norman French and many other foreign elements.

No one can listen long to a conversation between two natives of India in their own tongue, without hearing a large number of English words employed. In the vernacular press many English words are used to express the legal, political, and social usages of Europe and the discoveries of Western science. In some few cases a new application of an old vernacular term, or a new combination of vernacular words, is used to express the new object of thought. Thus we have *bijli ki batti* (lightning lamp) for electric light, and *vilayeti pani* (European water) for soda water, *ag gari* (fire carriage) for railway train, and *tar*, which literally means wire, is used to express the telegraph, or a telegram. But in the immense majority of cases English words are used in the vernaculars to express things and ideas imported from Europe. Naturally most of the English words thus adopted into the Indian vernaculars are more or less altered in sound, so that they may be pronounced more easily by Indian lips. The English tendency is to throw the accent back as far as possible. This is why we have, in English, "grámmar" and "cóurage," corresponding to the French *grammáire* and *couráge*, and, from the same inclination, we transform the Indian *tappál* and *hamál* into "táppal" and "hámal." But this tendency to have the accent as near the beginning of a word as possible, is as repugnant to the natives of India as it is to many other foreigners. Hence arises, in English words employed in Indian vernaculars, a displacement of accents just the reverse of that which often happens when an Indian word is uttered by Englishmen. If a Bombay tramcar conductor is asked to give a ticket for the Municipal Office, he will generally reply interrogatively "Municipál?" and you will scarcely get your ticket without conforming to his mispronunciation and placing the accent on the final syllable. In the same way, by misplacement of the accent, "hospital" is changed into *ispitál,* "towel" into *towál* and "captain" into *captán.* Sometimes a consonant is added through laziness. In some parts of England "gown" is pronounced "gownd," and the Anglo-Saxon *thunor* was enlarged into "thunder" in English, because, after pronouncing "n," the organs of speech are in such a convenient position for pronouncing "d," that it is less trouble to pronounce than to repress that sound. It is in exactly the same way that governor has come to be spelt and pronounced *govundar* in Indian vernaculars.

Etymologists have invented various terms to express the different ways in which words are modified for convenience of pronunciation. The process by which consonants of a different kind are replaced by consonants of the same kind is called assimilation. We have an instance of this kind of corruption in the conversion of "lemonade" into *limlet,* and of "flannel" into *falalin.* In both cases the word is changed, so that "l," instead of another consonant, may follow "l," just as in English, or rather in the Latin from which the English word is derived, "con" and "lateral" combine, not into "conlateral," but into "collateral." In other cases the opposite kind of change, called dissimilation, takes place, as when "champagne" is changed into *simkin*, because Indian lips find a difficulty in pronouncing the two labials "m" and "p" in such close proximity. To avoid the same combination of letters in the opposite order, "midshipman" used to be pronounced *meechilman*. Sometimes, to make the pronunciation easier, a new syllable is added, and thus "glass," "box," "tax," "constable," are changed into *gilas*, *bokus*, *tekus*, and *canas-table*. The last instance is peculiarly interesting, as, by the operation of two corruptions which cancel each other, the word has got back eventually to a much earlier form. "Constable" is derived originally from the Latin *comes stabuli*, companion, or count of the stable. In Norman French these two words combined into the one quadrisyllabic word, *conestable*, which in English, by the operation of syncope was reduced to "constable." Finally the native of India, to make the word suit his organs of speech, enlarges it again to *canas-table*, and so produces a word which is almost identical in sound with that used by William the Conqueror and his barons.

Another common instance of this corruption by addition of an extra syllable is the insertion of a vowel before words beginning with st and sc. Such words are always hard to pronounce. There is a town in the South West of Scotland called Stranraer. The children in the neighbourhood find it much easier to make this name begin with an I, and call it Istranraer. On the same principle, when the French formed derivatives from the Latin *stare,* they put a supporting vowel at the beginning of the words; and that is how we find in English "estate" and "establish" side by side with "state" and "stablish." These parallels may be a sufficient excuse for the uneducated Indian cook who proposes to make his master an *eestew,* and for the vernacular paper that describes the trials in the *ismal-cas-corut,* but scarcely for an educational institution not fifty miles from Bombay, that I saw some years ago proclaiming itself to the world on a printed board as an Anglo-Vernacular *Eescool.* Yet, after all, *eescool* in India is the result of the same philological process that produced *école* in France and *ysgol* in Wales.

In other cases the corruption, instead of adding a new syllable, diminishes the existing number of syllables by contraction, called syncope by philologists. This has already been illustrated above in the history of the word "constable," and we all know that "damsel" is short for *damosel*. In just the same way, "pantaloon" and "man-of-war" are shortened by natives of India into *pátloon* and *manwár*.

In the last-mentioned case the corruption is probably due to the common tendency to give foreign words a more familiar sound, of which we have quoted so many instances in the corruption of Indian words used by Englishmen. *Manwar* is much more like a Hindustani or Marathi noun than "man-of-war," of which it is a contraction. A clearer case is the corruption of the originally Mexican word "tomato" into *tambotu*, which, in Gujarathi, as I am told, means a milk pail.

This kind of corruption is specially common in the case of English proper names. The hill station of Matheran near Bombay supplies us with several instances that were recorded in its local paper, *Matheran Jottings*, in May, 1892. Panorama Point, the name of the finest point of view on Matheran Hill, is corrupted into Pandurang Point, and thus the long word of Greek origin is shortened into a very common Hindu name. In like manner the inhabitants of the hill have converted Porcupine

Point into Palkhi Point, although that name would be equally appropriate to any other of the Points to which the groaning Palkhiwalas bear their burdens. A house was built at Matheran by, or for, a Mr. Rogers. It was first, no doubt, called Rogersthan, or Roger's Place, but is now only known as Rajusthan, the Place of the King. This name, however, being a hybrid, ought, strictly speaking, to have been treated at an earlier point of our investigations, when we were considering words of mixed origin. English surnames are specially liable to be strangely altered in this way. "Kinloch" is corrupted into *tin lakh* (three lacs), a name agreeably suggestive of wealth. Mackenzie becomes Makkhanji, a compound of *makkhan*, butter, and *ji*, an honorary affix. Frere, Moore, Shaw, are converted respectively into *Fer*, meaning distance, *Mor*, a peacock, and *Shah*, a king. Jackson is disguised as *Jaykisn*, a Gujarathi compound of *jai*, victory, and *Krishn*, Krishna. Additional examples of the same kind of corruption are kindly given me by the *Hindi Punch*, from which I may quote the transformation of "Captain Gwyn" into *Govind Sahib*, and of "Who comes there," into *Hookum durr*.

Sometimes, strange to say, one English word or syllable is corrupted into another. Thus the last syllable of Mackintosh is corrupted into "toast," which following the corruption of the first two syllables into *makkhan*, butter, produces a combination more harmonious from a gastronomic than from a philosophical point of view. The Hon. Mr. Peile, now Sir James Peile, was always known in Western India as Appeal Sahib. The English word "appeal" was familiar in the law courts, and there was, perhaps, an underlying idea that Mr. Peile was somehow connected, in his official position, with the settlement of appeals. A similar instance is the corruption of the name Ravenscroft, belonging to another Bombay Member of Council. The name was a hard one, but reminded the uneducated Bombay native of the better known name of Crawford, which he had been compelled to master when the Crawford markets were built. This being the case, he determined not to take the trouble of mastering a new and difficult English name. So he tacked on the qualifying word "revenue," familiar as the name of a government department, before the name Crawford, and Mr. Ravenscroft was transformed into Revenue Crawford Sahib, as if he were a newly-discovered species of the genus Crawford.

We have next to consider a large number of English words that have acquired new meanings in

India. As their number is large, it is advisable to divide them into two classes for separate consideration. Let us first examine those English words which have changed their meaning by being used by natives of India, and secondly those which are applied to strange uses by the English themselves, although it may be difficult in one or two cases to be sure that we are assigning each particular word to its right class.

The two principal ways in which words change their meaning in the course of time is by generalisation and specialisation. Generalisation is the extension of a name to a larger class of objects, as when "solecism," which originally meant bad Greek spoken at the town of Soli in Asia Minor, came to include all cases of the violation of the grammar or idiom of any language; specialisation is the restriction of a name to a smaller class, as when the term "voyage," which used to mean a journey by land or sea, was restricted to journeys by sea. Both processes are illustrated by the following story. A friend of mine was travelling on official work in the Berars, and had to get provisions from the headmen of the villages through which he passed. One day his butler came and told him that the village patel was impudent and refused to supply provisions. The patel, on being called up, said: "I was not impudent; but the butler demanded brandy, and I have none." The butler replied: "I did not ask for brandy, but wine. I must have wine." His astonished master asked him what in the world he meant by demanding wine. "Must have wine," replied the butler; "can't make bread without wine." It turned out that what he wanted was yeast, and then the misunderstanding was at an end. It will be noticed that in the above conversation at cross purposes, the butler had, by the process of generalisation, extended the meaning "wine," so as to make it include everything fermented, while the patel, by the opposite process of specialisation, had understood "wine" to mean one particular alcoholic liquor, namely brandy. The tendency to generalisation is very common among native servants. They make the word "boot" include boots and shoes; call tarts, trifles, and sweet omelets indiscriminately pudding; apply the name "schoolmaster" to everyone connected with education, whether he teaches in a school or a college, or even if he is an inspector of schools or director of public instruction; and they make the word "office" do for their master's place of business, though it be a school, a college, or a law court. Specialisation is less common in the use of English words by Indians, although in the history of the English language it prevails more widely than generalisation. We see instances of it in the way in which Bombay servants narrow the meaning of "ticket" and "cover," and understand by these two words a postage stamp and an envelope. The word "sick" is used by natives to express every kind of illness, whether involving nausea or not. This, at first sight, looks like generalisation, but it is more probably a case of the preservation of the older and wider meaning of the word that prevailed when Englishmen first came to India. In like manner it has been often noticed that many Americanisms, for instance, the use of "rare" in the sense of underdone, and of "fall" in the sense of autumn, are really survivals of the meanings that English words had in the days of Queen Elizabeth and the Stuart Kings, when the American colonies were founded. Among the old meanings of words retained in America is this very use of the word "sick" in the wider sense, with which we are so familiar in India.

We come last to English words that are used in unusual senses, or in new combinations, by Englishmen living in India. Some express the amusements by which the Englishman tries to while away the years of his exile, such as tent-pegging, pig-sticking, and sky races. In pig-sticking the verb "stick" is used in a sense which has become obsolete. We now speak, not of sticking an animal with a spear, but of sticking a spear into an animal. The use of "stick" in this old sense points to the amusement and its name having originated many years ago, in the earlier days of English settlement in India; and in fact we find, in the supplement of *Hobson Jobson*, mention of the sport of pig-sticking as early as 1679, though it is not called by that name in the passage quoted. The verb "jink," so often applied to the boar in descriptions of boar hunts, is a Scotch word, used by Burns, from which we may infer that some early enthusiast in the introduction of the sport was a Scotchman, and that his influence was so great, that he gave a Scotch tinge to its technical language. One is also tempted to claim a Scotch origin for "dispense room." Certainly there is a good old Scotch word "spence," meaning provision room, which may be found in Scott's novels. In the description of Donald Bean's stronghold in *Waverley*, for instance, we read how "in one large aperture, which the robber facetiously called his spence (or pantry), there hung by the heels the carcasses of a sheep, or ewe, and two cows lately slaughtered." But if the Scotch "spence" had been attempted by native lips, it would almost certainly have been corrupted into "eespence," whereas the word in use is not "eespense" but "dispense." Therefore, we must rather derive it from the Portuguese word *despensa*, or the French word *despense*, both of which have the same meaning and etymology as the Scotch "spence." The spelling would seem to have been altered by English writers from "des" to "dis" in order to connect the word with the verb "dispense," because in the dispense room the Madamsahib dispenses household necessaries to the cook and butler. Of the derivation of "sky races," it is difficult to give a plausible conjecture. As they are usually held in the uncertain weather of the monsoon, it has been suggested that they may be races dependent on the sky, that is, on the state of the weather. Perhaps the name may have some connection with sky-larking, or with Norwegian sky-racing, which means racing with snow shoes on the *sky* or snow.

Of the names of Anglo-Indian dishes we may take first the familiar "country captain," the origin of which is satisfactorily explained by Yule. "Country," in India, is used adjectivally to express Indian, as opposed to European. Thus we have such expressions as a country-bred horse, country leather. Just as the Black Prince was so called because his armour was black, so by a similar transference of epithet, a country captain is prim arily a captain of a country ship, that is of a ship engaged in the Indian coasting trade, and secondarily, it comes to mean a favourite dish frequently provided for the captains of such vessels. The origin of "spatch cock" is much more puzzling. Yule and Whitworth do not find room for it in their dictionaries. But surely it is an Anglo-Indian term, for, if you were to ask for a spatch cock in a London hotel, or English village inn, the waiter would probably stare at you in blank amazement. It is commonly explained as a cock or hen suddenly despatched. This is the meaning, but can hardly be the derivation. For "spatch cock" or "spitch cock" is an old English word used by writers of the time of Shakespeare to express a way of cooking eels. King, the poetical chaplain of James I., used the word as a verb in the following lines :—

> "No man lards salt pork with orange peel
> Or garnishes his lamb with spitchcockt eel,"

and another writer employs the word as a noun, seemingly to express an eel cooked in this way. But in what way? Johnson in his dictionary says that to spitch-cock an eel is to cut him in pieces and roast him. From all this we may fairly conclude that the word had originally nothing to do with either "despatch" or "cock." The first syllable may be derived from "spit," as indicated by the old spelling "spitch cock," and still more by the spelling of Sir Thomas Browne, who speaks of a dish of "spits-cocked scorpions," or it may, perhaps, be from the French *dépecer*, cut in pieces, spelt in old French *despecher*. The second syllable is probably the passive participle of the verb cook, which in old English writers has only one "o," and may have been pronounced "cockt." Thus the derivative meaning in either case would mean split in small pieces and cooked, for, in order that small pieces of meat may be conveniently roasted, they must first be spitted together. The old derivation being forgotten, and a false derivation being invented which gave the word a new meaning, the spitch cock, which had been a spitch-cockt eel to our ancestors, changed its character and became an Anglo-Indian spatch cock.

"Chummery" is a useful noun which appears to have been coined in Bombay to express a bungalow in which two or three persons chum together. Murray only quotes one instance of the word, but not in its concrete Anglo-Indian sense. The author quoted is Besant, the novelist, who speaks of persons living together "in bachelor chummery," but in this quotation the absence of the article shows that "chummery" is an abstract term, meaning the state of being chums. Another social word that, perhaps, originated in Bombay, is the term "first lady," applied to the lady at a dinner party, who is taken in to dinner by the host. This post carries with it the important duty of making the first move to break up the party, and, when the guest chosen as first lady is a young bride new to India and unacquainted with this peculiar social usage, complications arise, and the party may remain unbroken to an unconscionably late hour, everybody waiting for the bride to take her departure first. In Bengal the verb "cart" has acquired a new social meaning. It means, or used to mean, to drive a young lady out in a cart, or carriage. Such conduct is understood to imply matrimonial intentions, and is considered tantamount to an engagement. This use of "cart" will be found in Bellew's *Memoirs of a Griffin.* Why a new arrival in India is called a griffin, would be hard to say. A griffin is a strange composite beast, between a lion and an eagle, and, perhaps, the idea is that the new comer is a similarly composite creature, as he has left Europe and not yet been thoroughly initiated into the mysteries of Anglo-Indian life. Some Anglo-Indian colloquialisms are grimly jocular, such as "peg," according to one etymology, and "promotion nuts." It will probably never be decided whether pegs are so called because they screw you up when you are low, or because each adds a peg to your coffin, or because old-fashioned drinking vessels were measured by pegs. Possibly, as has been suggested to me, the word may have an Indian derivation from *pej*, a Marathi word meaning a draught of rice and water, often taken by natives in the early morning. The most probable explanation is, however, that given by an old soldier, who remembers that drinks in the canteen used to be scored up by fixing pegs in a board. This being the case, the symbol might have come by metonymy to be used for the thing symbolised, and "Give me another peg" would come to be regarded as a natural equivalent for "Give me another drink." The term "promotion nuts," applied to the cashew nuts on account of their indigestibility, is an indication of the official character of Anglo-Indian society, which makes its junior members cynically regard their seniors as so many obstacles in the way of promotion. The appreciation of the advantages enjoyed by the members of the covenanted civil service is expressed by the term "twice-born," applied to them. "Twice-born" is a literal translation of *dvija*, the adjective that distinguishes the three higher Hindu castes, the members of which are born again at the time of their investiture with the sacred cord. Grass-cutter is another literal translation of an Indian term, unless it may be regarded as a corruption of its equivalent *ghāskātā,* in which case it should have been mentioned earlier, as being not of English, but Indian, origin. To "cut pay" is a new verbal combination made in India to give a literal rendering of the Indian idiom *puggar katna,* which, if not translated thus into what may be called dog English, would require rather more words to express its meaning. "Man-eater," specialised in the sense of man-eating tiger, "native town," and "fire temple," are three more combinations of English words which acquire in India special meanings. "Home," as used by the Englishman in India, almost always means England as opposed to the land of his exile, and this usage has become so inveterate, that even natives of this country, when they contemplate a visit to Europe, may be heard telling their friends that they are "going home."

Among the new words which the Englishman adds to his vocabulary in the East, some of the commonest are of Portuguese derivation. The large number of these Portuguese words is a visible proof of the former extent and power of the Portuguese dominion in India. It would, however, be out of place for me to try and trace them to their origin, when we have in India Portuguese scholars so much better fitted for the task. I have, indeed, felt that it was quite venturesome enough, in one so imperfectly acquainted with the vernaculars of India as I am, to discuss the words of Indian origin which are daily on our lips in this country. However, by availing myself freely of the vernacular knowledge possessed by my pupils at Elphinstone College, and by consulting the literary labours of those who have studied deeply the languages of India, and have given to the world the result of their studies, it has been possible for me to supply the defects of my own very imperfect acquaintance with Oriental languages. It has been my main object to show that the same principles of philology that rule the formation of the great literary languages of the world are clearly exemplified even in such a humble hybrid dialect as Anglo-Indian. If I have succeeded at all in my endeavour, I must express in the fullest way my obligations to the Anglo-Indian dictionaries of Col. Yule and of Mr. Whitworth of the Bombay Civil Service, without the abundant material supplied in whose works, it would have been impossible for me to put together these few tentative remarks on Anglo-Indian words and phrases.

Heredity and the Regeneration of India.

THE sphere of the law of heredity extends over all animate existence. The law that like produces like prevails over the generations not only of animals, but also of plants. In treating the question a distinction must be made between specific and individual heredity. Specific heredity, the law that plants and animals of one species cannot produce plants and animals of another species, that the seed of the oak cannot develop into a beech tree, and that a lion cannot be the parent of a tiger, is so invariable that, like the law of universal causation and the succession of night and day, it excites neither the wonder nor even the notice of unreflective minds, who see nothing remarkable in the normal course of nature and irrationally reserve their wonder for the exceptional and uncommon. When we pass from specific to individual heredity, the operation of the law becomes less clearly recognisable, because more liable to be defeated by counteracting causes. Though we are certain that the offspring of human parents must be a human being, we may expect, but cannot be sure, that a child will inherit most of the peculiar characteristics of mind and body, by which its parents were distinguished from other human beings. This is, however, just what might have been expected from the operation of the law of heredity. We have to remember that, though by the law of heredity, men's physical and mental characteristics are mainly determined by their parents, they may be influenced in a less degree by grandparents and more remote ancestors. Being the descendants of countless generations of human beings, we have no ancestors from whom to inherit the nature of tigers and horses. But, though our parents may have one set of individual characteristics, we may inherit a large admixture of opposite characteristics from a grandfather. Thus Edward III. resembled not his father Edward II., but his able and warlike grandfather. Yet, on the whole, children are more likely to resemble their parents than their grandparents. According to Galton, we inherit about 1-16th of our original nature from our grandparents and a whole quarter from our parents. For the sake of simplicity, confining our attention to inheritance from parents, we can say with regard to individual characteristics that children tend to resemble their parents, that the child of virtuous parents is more likely to be virtuous than the child of vicious parents, and the children of parents strong in mind and body are likely under ordinary circumstances to grow up into men and women strong in mind and body. The truth of this, as a general rule, is so obvious, that it has been recognised from the earliest times of which we have any record. Moral heredity is recognised in the laws of Manu, where we read, "A woman always brings into the world a son gifted with the same qualities as he who begat him," and "We may know by his act the man that belongs to a low class, or who is born of a disreputable mother," and again, "A man of low birth has the evil dispositions of his father or his mother, or of both—he never can hide his descent." The anciently established caste system of India and of Egypt is a recognition on an immense scale of heredity, for its chief justification is that physical and mental aptitudes for work are handed down from generation to generation, that the descendant of many generations of carpenters starts life with an inherited capacity for working in wood, so that it would be in most cases a waste of talent to educate him to any other trade. Another practical illustration of the belief in the principle of heredity is to be found in Japan, where, it is said, the parents of criminals are punished for the crimes of their children. The proverbs of all nations recognise the resemblance between parents and children. In England, a son resembling his father is proverbially declared to be a "chip of the old block." An Indian proverb tells us that "a son takes after his father as the fruit of the banyan tree is like the tree on which it grows." Quotations in support of heredity might be collected from most of the great writers of ancient and modern times. Aristotle illustrated it by the story of a father, who, being dragged out of the house by his son, besought that son to drag him no farther than the threshold, for, he said, "I in my day dragged my father no farther than the threshold." The grim humour of this story is reproduced in Browning's poem of *Halbert and Hob.* But it is useless to accumulate the various expressions of belief in heredity to be found in the writings and sayings of all ages. Enough has been said to illustrate how widely the principle has been accepted as true by the wisdom of the ancients.

It may, however, be objected that many generalizations, once widely accepted, have had to be rejected by modern science, as based upon no better foundation than a certain number of affirmative instances, that by their strange coincidence attracted attention, while the contrary instances, having nothing remarkable in them, were easily forgotten. As Bacon clearly pointed out, all the old superstitious beliefs in astrology, witchcraft, charms, omens, and all kinds of magic were due to this tendency of the human mind to attend to positive instances and neglect the duty of searching for negative instances. Can the same be said of the principle of heredity? Can we believe that it is based only on a few chance cases in which children happened to resemble their parents, and could we find, if we looked for them, just as large a proportion of instances of resemblance between men born, say, in the same year, or in the same house, as between parents and children? If this were so, then this generalization, like the superstitions of the ignorant, must be condemned as a popular delusion for which there is no rational foundation. This, however, is very far from being the case. Modern science, instead of attacking the belief in heredity, confirms it on rational grounds. Specific heredity, the law that animals can only reproduce their own species, is of such universal necessity that it admits of no exception. Indeed, the universality of specific heredity is a very strong argument in favour of individual heredity. Seeing that through the whole animal and vegetable world, parents of one species can never produce offspring of another species, it is natural to expect that parents who transmit all their specific qualities should also transmit some of their individual peculiarities also. You have probably all got in your own experience instances of the resemblance between parents and children in private life, that are far too striking and numerous to be attributable to chance. Writers upon the subject of heredity in collecting statistics have to confine themselves to the relationships of eminent men, whose characters are known from history, so that readers may test the accuracy of their instances. Even from this limited range of selection Galton and Ribot can bring forward a convincing array of instances It would be useless for me here to bring all this great mass of evidence before you. Let me, however, as good typical modern instances of intellectual heredity, direct your attention to the amount of literary talent and learning that has been displayed by two English families—the Arnolds and the Wordsworths—in both which cases I happen to be able to supplement the information attainable in biographical dictionaries by my own individual experience. The literary reputation of the Arnold family appears to begin with Thomas Arnold, headmaster of Rugby, whose history of Rome deserves to be regarded as one of the very greatest masterpieces of English prose. His eldest son was Matthew Arnold, the poet; a younger son was W. D. Arnold, Director of Public Instruction in the Punjab, author of *Oakfield*, whose death is consecrated in one of his brother's most beautiful and pathetic poems. The second son of Thomas Arnold was another Thomas Arnold, who has written several works on English literature. His daughter is Mrs. Ward, the authoress of *Robert Elsmere*. One of his sons, who was my contemporary at school, won scholarships there and at Oxford by his marked superiority in English over other candidates. The only original work, as far as I know, that he has yet produced, is his treatise on the *Roman System of Provincial Administration*, by which he won the Arnold Essay at Oxford; but he may be expected in the future fully to sustain the family literary reputation. The literary talent and genius manifested in the Wordsworth family is equally remarkable. The great poet's sister Dorothy is known to have rivalled him in poetic insight and keen susceptibility to the beauties of nature

His brother was the Rev. Christopher Wordsworth, Master of Trinity College, Cambridge, and author of *Ecclesiastical Biographies.* Two sons of the Rev. Christopher Wordsworth became Bishops, one the Bishop of St. Andrews, the other the Bishop of Lincoln. The Bishop of St. Andrews wrote a work on the Bible in Shakespeare. His younger brother, the Bishop of Lincoln, is the author of *Grecce Pictorial and Descriptive,* and many other learned works. One of the Bishop of Lincoln's sons, whose lectures I had the privilege of attending at Brasenose College, Oxford, has since become Bishop of Salisbury, making the third Bishop in the Wordsworth family. He is an eminent Latin scholar and is the author of *Fragments of Early Latin.* His brother, Canon Wordsworth, wrote *Social Life in the English Universities.* His sister is joint authoress of a biography of her father the Bishop of Lincoln. If we now turn to the direct line of descent from the poet we find it well represented by the late Principal of Elphinstone College, whose literary talents and poetic genius are well known in Bombay and deserve to be better known by the world.

Two such instances of family genius I only give as examples. They would prove little in themselves if they were not supported by the large array of similar instances, far too numerous to be included in this short paper, of hereditary genius collected by Galton from his investigations into the family history of eminent judges, statesmen, commanders, men of science, poets, musicians, painters, and orators. Our own personal experience makes it plain to us that, as might be expected, bodily strength, moral character, and ordinary intellectual ability are as distinctly hereditary as genius. We may, therefore, safely conclude that the intellectual and moral character and the physical strength with which a child begins life are entirely, or almost entirely, derived from its parents. It may perhaps be objected that in many cases healthy parents have unhealthy children and wise parents have foolish children. This, of course, cannot be denied. But such exceptions are quite compatible with the fact that the children of healthy parents are more likely to be healthy than the children of unhealthy parents, and that the children of wise parents are more likely to be wise than the children of unwise parents. In the case of large numbers—for instance, if we consider whole nations instead of individual instances—the exceptions due to chance or counteracting cases would disappear. Just as a thousand picked marksmen would be sure to make a better score at the target than a thousand men unskilled in the use of the rifle, although one or two of the best shots made by the unskilled riflemen might happen to be better than one or two of the worst shots of the picked marksmen, so, other circumstances remaining the same, the next generation of a nation of parents strong in mind and body is sure to be stronger in mind and body than the offspring of a nation of mentally and physically weak parents.

Having thus established that the bodily and mental powers of children are to a very large extent determined by the bodily and mental health of their parents, it is natural next to inquire whether a child derives more of its original character from its father or its mother, and whether any distinction can be made between the inheritance derived from the two parents. Schopenhauer was strongly of opinion that a distinction could be made between the mental gifts derived from father and mother. He was firmly convinced that a child derives its intellect from its mother and its will from its father. The same distinction is drawn in the *Vedanga-nirukla*, a Sanskrit medical work, in which we are told that the child derives from the mother his brains and other passive elements, but from his father his strength and active powers. If this were so, it would be expedient in the interests of the coming generation to cultivate especially the intellects of girls and the will power of boys. But in this as in other cases Schopenhauer seems to have generalized for the most part from his own instance. As he happened himself to inherit his intellect from a clever mother, and Goethe and many other eminent men are known to have resembled him in this, he elevated this order of mental succession into a general rule, ignoring the equally numerous cases of men who, like William Pitt, Hartley Coleridge, and J. S. Mill, inherited their intellect from their fathers. However numerous the instances we examine, it seems impossible to accept any such distinction as Schopenhauer believes to exist between the kind of influence, that male and female parents have upon the mind of their offspring. As far as can be seen, it appears that father and mother both have a share in affecting all the elements of their offspring's character by hereditary transmission, the will, the intellect, the emotions, and the sensations. In some cases a child may inherit more of its father's will and its mother's intellect, another child may inherit more of its father's intellect and its mother's will, a third may inherit an intellect and will about half-way between the intellects and wills of its two parents. Nor can any distinction be made between the quantity of hereditary influence exerted by fathers and mothers over their sons, on the one hand, and their daughters on the other. Although the code of Manu and the author of the *Vedanga-nirukla,* as we have seen, fully acknowledge the fact that sons inherit their character from their mother as well as from their father, it is, I believe, the prevalent opinion in India that sons resemble their fathers and daughters their mothers. But many eminent European physiologists have held the opposite theory of cross heredity, that daughters take after their fathers, and sons after their mothers. Michelet the historian calls this a "law of which history has but few exceptions." It has been called in to explain the fact that so many great men have ordinary sons. Ribot, the French psychologist, is inclined to believe that cross heredity has fewer exceptions than heredity in the same sex. But an impartial examination of statistics seems to give no decided preponderance to either of these two opposing theories, so that we are naturally driven to the conclusion that mothers and fathers exert an equal influence upon the original groundwork of character, with which the boys and girls of the next generation commence life.

It is at this point that we are in a position to apply the doctrine of heredity to the question of the regeneration of India. Why is it that India, which in the golden ages of Sanskrit literature was in the forefront of the world's civilization, has been for the last thousand years in a backward condition, while other nations have been progressing rapidly and far outstripping her in the race? Why is it that the nation, that in the past produced poetry and philosophy fit to rival the masterpieces of Greece, has for so many centuries produced no literary work of high rank, no great poet, or dramatist, or historian, or philosopher, no great name in literature since the days of Sanskrit literature, no man of first-rate eminence in practical life since Akbar, and even he, though an Indian by birth, belonged to a family but newly settled in India? No single cause can account for this strange retrogression, but I am convinced that the consideration of heredity plainly shows that the principal cause has been the introduction of the practice of female seclusion, which appears to have gradually become more prevalent and stringent from the date of the earliest Aryan invasion of India, and came to a climax at the time of the Mahomedan conquest. If you accept the law of heredity—and I think you cannot refuse to accept it—the practice of female seclusion must constantly tend to national deterioration, to diminution of physical, intellectual, and probably also moral strength in each successive generation. Intellectual and physical strength are equally dependent on active outdoor exercise for their development and establishment. Strict female seclusion prevents the mothers, that is, half the parents of each succeeding generation, from exercising their minds and bodies, except in the feeblest manner. What physical exercise, worthy of the name, can be enjoyed by secluded women, who are never allowed to breathe the free air of heaven on foot or on horseback, and even when they can afford the luxury of what is called by a misnomer carriage exercise, have the air excluded by blinds and curtains? Equally little mental exercise is afforded to women confined entirely to domestic duties indoors, and having no opportunity of taking any part whatever in the active life of their husbands and brothers. The consequence of this mode of life is that a girl grows up to womanhood with her mind and body imperfectly developed, and transmits, as far as in her lies, her own weakness of mind and body to her children.

Let us try to put the matter more clearly by expressing in a numerical form the way in which female seclusion tends to make each generation weaker in mind and body than its predecessor. Let us imagine a nation in which female seclusion is the invariable rule, and suppose that the average man at the time of marriage has had his mind and body well developed by a good education, including the experience obtained by active outdoor life. Let us express his mental and bodily strength by the number ten, and say that he has 10° of mental and bodily strength. Assuming that the average woman is somewhat inferior in bodily and mental strength to the average man, we may suppose that the average woman in this nation was capable of being developed by a good education to 8° of mental and bodily strength, but that, owing to seclusion, her mind and body were so imperfectly exercised that at the time of marriage her mental and bodily strength was only 6°. Thus we have an average father of 10° and an average mother of 6° of mental and bodily strength, so that by the principle of heredity the average child of the next generation may be expected to be born with a capability of being developed by good education to the amount of capacity midway between that of the father 10°, and that of the mother 6°—that is, to 8°, the arithmetical mean between 10° and 6°. Making the same distinction as before between male and female capacity, we may say that the average man of the next generation will be developed by a good education to 9° of capacity, and the average woman, though capable of being developed to 7°, will, owing to female seclusion, be only developed to 5°. When the men and women of this generation marry, the average child will only be of 7° of capacity, whereas but for female seclusion the average child of each successive generation would have had 9° of capacity. If any one takes the trouble to follow up this calculation, he will see that in this way female seclusion, by stunting the mental and bodily development of the mothers of each generation, tends to produce steady deterioration as time goes on. Though this tendency, like many other tendencies, may be counteracted by other opposing circumstances, it is just as likely to be aggravated by other causes acting in the same direction, so that it is natural to expect that any nation that adopts female seclusion will deteriorate steadily in intellectual and bodily strength.

On the whole, I think, we shall find that this conclusion deduced from the law of heredity is confirmed by the experience of history, so far as historical facts with their complex intermixture of causes and effects can give support to any law of cause and effect. At any rate, historical facts harmonise with the conclusion. The rapid rise and fall of great Oriental empires may be mainly attributed to the effect of female seclusion. The usual history of Oriental empires is that they originate in some poor tribe or nation overpowering a wealthy monarchy and taking its place for a time, only to be displaced after an interval of wealth and prosperity by some other race of poor conquerors, who go through the same cycle of conquest, prosperity and decay. The history of Europe shows that wealth and prosperity does not necessarily lead to national weakness. The decay of power of the great monarchies of the East may more naturally be attributed to the practice of female seclusion rendered possible by wealth, and making the nation that adopts it an easy prey to poor enemies, whose poverty and nomad life have prevented them from adopting the custom. I imagine that it was thus that the hardy Marathas, who seem to have allowed their women more share in active outdoor life than is usual in India, were able to wreck the Mogul power. The same explanation may be given of the early Aryan conquest of India. The decreasing stringency of female seclusion, that we find as we go back by the help of Sanskrit literature towards the earliest times of Aryan India, indicates that the ancestors of the modern Hindus allowed their women in Central Asia the same freedom that is still enjoyed there among the nomad Koords in spite of their Mahometanism. Thus the early Aryan conquerors of India and the men of genius, who endowed the world with Sanskrit literature, were the descendants of many generations, the women of which had been adapted by a free life to be the mothers of children strong in mind and body, and so paved the way for a period of success in war and literature, rivalling the age of Elizabeth in England and the outburst of Athenian genius that followed and accompanied the Persian war. Perhaps only one Oriental parallel can be found to these great epochs of national history, and that in the conquests of the Arabians at the beginning of the Mahometan era, and the triumphs of literature and science that followed these conquests. The brilliant part that the Arabians then played in the history of the world is another fact harmonising with the view that female emancipation is conducive to national greatness, for, as Palgrave remarks in the account of his Arabian travels, "The absolute seclusion, which, it is well known, imprisons physically and morally the fair sex in orthodox Mahometan lands, is seldom, if ever, observed in Arabia, where women bear a great part in active life and domestic cares, keep shops, buy, sell, and sometimes even go to war." If so much freedom is now enjoyed by Arabian women, we may infer, and the ancient poetry of idolatrous Arabia supports the inference, that they were still freer before Arabia was converted by Mahomet. So that there we have an instance of a nation, unenervated by the intense heat of the climate in which they lived, issuing forth to conquer a great part of the civilized world, and taking the leading position not only in arms, but also in science and literature; and the Oriental nation that effected this was one conspicuous for the breach of the custom of female seclusion. In course of time, when the later Arabians became rich enough to build harems for their wives and daughters, their valour and genius began to suffer decay. I must, however, before leaving the subject of these historical instances, again remind you that, owing to the vast complexity of the causes to which national success is due, they can only be expected to illustrate and verify, and not to prove, my position, which almost entirely rests on the indisputable fact that the mental and bodily power of children is to a large extent determined by the mental and bodily power of their mothers, and that the mothers of the next generation cannot be expected to be strong in body and vigorous in mind, if they are confined to a sedentary indoor life.

It may be objected that, even though the practice of seclusion may be prejudicial to the intellectual and physical strength of individuals and nations, it is nevertheless extremely valuable as a safeguard of moral virtue. It is, of course, perfectly true that seclusion defends women against temptations that they would encounter in an unsecluded life. But it must be remembered that the absence of temptation, though it may diminish the amount of actual wrong-doing, does not constitute virtue. A man with murderous or thievish inclinations is not necessarily made more virtuous by being imprisoned for life, though he may be thereby deprived of all opportunities of committing theft and murder. The highest virtue consists in facing and resisting and conquering temptations, not in fleeing from them. Although in some cases it may be a good thing that a man, who has some reason to distrust his own resolution, should retire from public life and its temptations, such cloistered virtue, as Bacon calls it, is far inferior to that of the brave man, who follows the rules of virtue in the midst of all the temptations of ordinary daily life. It is this struggle that, if successful, really strengthens the moral character, and it must be remembered that the power of resisting temptation is, like all other mental qualities, transmissible by heredity. So that every one who gains a moral victory makes the gaining of such victories easier in the future to his children and his children's children, and so paves the way for their moral progress to greater victories. But such training in militant virtue is denied to women by the practice of seclusion; and when they become mothers, they hand down to their children moral wills unstrengthened by exercise. In their own case, the want of power of resisting temptation would not perhaps so much matter, as it might be urged with some plausibility that it is useless to arm them against temptations to which they will never be exposed. Nor would the want be so material, if the law of heredity went by sex, and sons took after their fathers and daughters after their mothers. But there is no reason to believe this is the case, and some believers in heredity, as we have seen, actually on the contrary believe that sons rather take after their mothers and daughters after their fathers. Without accepting this extreme view, we have every reason to believe that sons derive at least as much of their original character from their mothers as from their fathers, so that the untrained moral will inherited from a mother bred up in seclusion may descend to her son, who is not, in like manner, protected against temptations to error, and thus falls an easy prey to the temptations of vice when he becomes his own master and goes out into the world.

Thus, even if there may be a certain amount of doubt as to the moral effects of seclusion on the women who are secluded, it is hardly possible to deny the bad moral effects it is likely to have on their sons by transmitting to them a character ill fitted to cope with temptation. If to this bad moral effect be added the gradual deterioration of intellectual and physical strength that seclusion tends to produce in each successive generation, it is clear, that any nation that adopts the practice of female seclusion is, to use a sporting phrase, severely handicapped in every kind of contest with nations that do not adopt this custom. A nation with this custom, when it competes with other nations for political, literary, scientific or any other kind of pre-eminence, may be compared to a gladiator fighting with one hand tied behind his back, who may by good luck gain temporary success, but can scarcely hope to be permanently victorious. Therefore, any true patriot, who sincerely wishes for the regeneration of India, and has any care for the future of his country, should try to further female emancipation by all means in his power, or else he will be guilty of the logical inconsistency of desiring the end and refusing to use the means. How the emancipation of women in the East is to be accomplished, is a question on which I can say nothing. There are, no doubt, immense obstacles in the way, the strength of which it is impossible for an outsider like me to appreciate; and all that can be said with certainty on the subject is that it must be very gradual. Attempts to introduce female emancipation suddenly are almost sure to defeat their own object. But until progress in this direction is somehow or other effected, general progress will be woefully retarded.

Some twenty-three centuries ago, the Athenian public assembly was discussing the fate of Mitylene, a revolted city that had been re-conquered. The Athenian demagogue Cleon proposed that all the men fit to bear arms should be slain, and that all the women and children should be sold into slavery. Another orator, called Diodotus, argued against this monstrous proposition. It is an extraordinary fact that in his whole speech, as reported by Thucydides, Diodotus makes no appeal to the compassionate feelings of his audience, and deliberately bases all his arguments on national interests and none on pity. I have followed the same course in urging the necessity of female emancipation. Had I been an orator, I might have attempted to draw a vivid picture of captives pining for liberty and freedom to live in the sunlight and breathe the free air of heaven. No doubt it would have been urged on the other side that custom reconciles women to a secluded life, as it prevents the canary bird from feeling its captivity. This counter argument is, however, not quite convincing. Those who bring it forward forget that girls must inherit from their fathers aspirations for a free life, and are allowed a short taste of freedom in their childhood. But I prefer to follow the example of Diodotus and base my argument entirely on national interests. Those of you who know me best, my own pupils who have wandered with me year after year through the mazes of Logic and Moral Philosophy, know that, as a rule, I am not a person of very decided opinions; that I am almost too prone to see both sides of every question. But as to the prejudicial effects of female seclusion upon the mental and bodily power of any nation or community, that adopts the custom, my conviction is so strong, that in urging the necessity of female emancipation as necessary to national progress, I feel justified in concluding my address, as Milton's Satan concluded his speech to his followers lying at his feet in the oblivious pool of Lethe, with the words :—

"Awake! arise! or be ever fallen."

Some Indian Proverbs.

ARCHBISHOP TRENCH in his interesting book on proverbs tries to show how national character is reflected in the sayings of various nations. His attempt is not entirely unsuccessful; but it must be always borne in mind that individual proverbs cannot by any means be assumed with certainty to express the opinions of the average members of the nation that produces them. Each proverb must certainly express the opinion of an immense number of men, but it may be the opinion of a strong minority protesting against some wrong opinion or practice dear to the nation as a whole. Thus it is that proverbs contradict each other. The Indian proverb, "To work without pay is better than sitting idle," is diametrically opposed to a Scotch proverb that says, "Better sit still than work for nought." May we conclude on this evidence that the native of India is much more industrious than the Scot? Certainly not. Both proverbs may express the opinions of minorities, and very likely further search would find Scotch proverbs condemning idleness as an evil in itself and Indian proverbs in praise of idleness. In order to find evidence of national character we require a large number of proverbs all pointing the same way, and we must have reason to believe that there are few or no contradictory instances.

If we thus guard ourselves against rash conclusions, we shall find that a general survey of the proverbs of all nations, although in some cases it indicates national peculiarities, much more conspicuously demonstrates similarity in character and experience between nations widely separated by large intervals of space and time. In spite of the immense difference in social manners and customs and in religion between England and India, most Indian proverbs have more or less exact equivalents in English and other languages. Mr. Roebuck in his collection of Oriental proverbs comments on the saying, "The miser who refuses at once is preferable to the liberal man who gives slowly," and expresses his belief "that the natives would in general be better satisfied with injustice administered at once than await the tedious decision of a cause." This may be true, but it does not reveal any peculiarity of Indian character. Just as this proverb in its general application is equivalent to the often quoted Latin proverb, "*Bis dat qui cito dat*" (He gives twice who gives quickly), so its special application to the law may be easily paralleled in Shakespeare's complaint of the "law's delay," which has found an echo in so many hearts that the phrase has become proverbial. In fact, on examination it will be found that the immense difference in religion and social life between India and England does not much affect the thought contained in the proverbs of the two nations, although it causes them to be illustrated by different kinds of examples. The difference is in most cases rather a difference of form than a difference in matter. To take a typical instance, exactly the same meaning is expressed by the English proverbial phrase, "Carry coals to Newcastle," and the Indian, "Sell a needle in the street where the blacksmiths work," although the latter uses as an illustration not the black diamond which is one of the chief sources of England's wealth, but the peculiarly Indian or Oriental custom by which all workmen of the same kind congregate together in the same streets or quarters of cities. Many equally close parallels will present themselves as we go on, and it will be difficult to find Indian proverbs which can be said directly to reveal peculiar traits in the character of the Indian people among an immense number of proverbs that throw much light on their manners and customs. Most of them only reveal national character indirectly, inasmuch as the existence of the manners and customs referred to in the proverbs gives evidence of the tastes and sentiments of the people.

There are, however, a few exceptions to this statement. The immense number of Indian proverbs regarding sugar as among the chief joys of this life illustrates clearly the almost universal love of sweetmeats that prevails among young and old throughout India. There is also a strikingly large number of proverbs that seem to indicate what Bacon calls morigeration—that is, submission or even servility to those in power, more than is approved by any expression of English proverbial philosophy. Take, for instance, the proverb that says that "A man in need calls even an ass his father," or in a slightly different form, "Even a wise man in need holds the feet of an ass"—that is, bows down before an ass and holds his feet in supplication. It would be hard to parallel this among English proverbs. Individual Englishmen may have given such precepts or approved such conduct. Bacon does not condemn Aristippus, the Greek exponent of the philosophy of morigeration, "when, having a petition to Dionysius and no ear given to him, he fell down at his feet; whereupon Dionysius stayed and gave him the hearing and granted it; and afterwards some person, tender on the behalf of philosophy, reproved Aristippus that he would offer the profession of philosophy such an indignity as for a private suit to fall at a tyrant's feet: but he answered *it was not his fault, but it was the fault of Dionysius that had his ears in his feet.*" "These and the like applications and stoopings to points of necessity and convenience," Bacon goes on to remark, "cannot be disallowed: for though they may have some outward baseness, yet in a judgment truly made they are to be accounted submissions to the occasion and not to the person." However the precepts in favour of morigeration given by Bacon were not sufficiently in accordance with the spirit of the average Englishman to have become proverbial Other Indian proverbs in accordance with Bacon's theory and practice are, "Never fight with one superior in wealth or strength," "If circumstances demand, we must call an ass our uncle." "He that is servile is the favourite of God," and "He that is servile will fill his belly." On the other hand it is but fair to mention the contradictory Indian proverbs opposed to morigeration. One of them holds up to scorn the man who is "a toady and nevertheless touches the tip of his nose with his tongue." This gesture is indicative of pride; and the proverb regards the toady as the last person in the world who has any right to feel self-satisfaction. "If you wish to retain your own honour, do not ask any one even for a draught of water," prescribes even excessive independence, as also does the saying that "A tiger never eats grass." The misery of a dependent life is well expressed by the common saying that "Dependence on another is perpetual disappointment." These maxims of independence show, that even if the past circumstances of India often led the people unduly to favour morigeration, there were always at least strong minorities who were opposed to such conduct and cherished in their hearts the love of individual liberty.

In considering the revelation of character by proverbs, we must not forget to record those which are either expressly intended to hit off the characteristics of various geographical or social sections of the people, or assume that these characteristics are well known beyond the reach of dispute. Many such may be found in England. "A Scottish man and a Newcastle grindstone travel all the world over," points to the travelling propensities of a people who, according to Dr. Johnson's epigrammatic remark, found in all their country no prospect so fair as that of the road leading to England. Other local proverbs given in Mr. Ray's collection ascribe faithlessness to the men of Dursley in Gloucestershire, and rudeness to the inhabitants of Hogs-Norton. The wise men of Gotham in England, and in Greece the inhabitants of Abdera, and the Bœotians, particularly those of Thebes, have been chosen as types of stupidity. Their Indian proverbial equivalents are the "Children of Budlaoon" in Rohilkund, whose reputation for stupidity is perhaps no better deserved than that earned by the Greek cities which produced Democritus, Protagoras, Epaminondas, Plutarch, and Pindar. According to another proverb Bhagulpoor is famous for hypocrites, Kuhulgaum for foot-pads, and Patna for bankrupts, while a third proverb reflecting on the inhabitants of individual towns tells us that "The people of Sialkote are thoroughly wicked." Turning now to proverbs that deal with larger collections of people, we find one declaring that "The Brahmin is short-sighted, the Banya long-sighted, and the Shudra rash." Another proverb that attempts to distinguish the leading characteristics of large divisions of the native community, says that "A Parsee is wise after the event, a Banya is prudent, a Borah is meek, a Mahometan blood-thirsty" Of two other proverbs mentioning the Parsee, one declares that his blow is like a cannon ball. This, at first sight, seems rather a strange thing to be said of a community that is generally supposed to be peace-loving and has for many generations had no chance of displaying martial valour. It is, however, supported by the enthusiasm with which the Parsees of to-day have taken up cricket and other active English games. This indicates that they have really kept up since the time of their immigration to India the physical strength and energy of their warlike ancestors. Another proverb tells us that "A Parsee turns round in no time," which is a less pleasing Hindu estimate of Parsee character. There are also, as might be expected, several Hindu proverbs reflecting injuriously upon the Mahometans. They are purposely expressed in Hindustani, the language of the Indian Mahometans, so that they profess to condemn the Mahometans out of their own mouth. Thus, "Is there anyone to fight? Yes, I and my brother," is put in Hindustani as a dialogue typical of Mahometan quarrelsomeness. "Yours is mine, and mine is—— " ends with an expressive aposiopesis, which is intended to express that the Mahometan's ideal of mutual goodwill is not strictly impartial. The proverbial estimate of the Pathan character seems to be that it has great possibilities for good or evil. "The son of a Pathan," it is said, "is sometimes a saint and sometimes a devil!" The Englishman has hardly been long enough in the country to find a place in Indian proverbs. There is, however, one proverb which has for its subject-matter the characteristics of English rule, and, therefore, gives indirectly a popular Indian estimate of English character. "Under the British raj," it is said, "the gods have gone away to the mountains, the pious Mahometans to Mecca, and a dher (man of low caste) jostles you."

Among the most interesting of Indian proverbs are those which throw light on domestic manners and customs. Several proverbs indicate the oppression endured by the young bride at the hands of her mother-in-law. "In the month of Posh the mother-in-law is very angry while the wife is contented." The explanation of this is that Posh falls in winter when the working day is short, so that the poor hard-worked little wife gets grateful rest from her labours, while the mother-in-law cannot enjoy the pleasure of working her hard except for a limited number of hours. But, unfortunately, the number of the days in the month of Posh are limited, and the young bride has so few happy days in her year that an Indian equivalent for the English, "Every dog has his day," is, "If there are a hundred days for the mother-in-law, there must be, at least, one for the daughter-in-law." A similar contrast between the position of the two is made by the proverbial saying, "Get a daughter-in-law and take rest. Let me spin and you grind the grain." One merciful proverb puts into the mouth of the daughter-in-law entering her husband's house the pathetic appeal, "Mother-in-law, do not use me ill. There is one before you to be exposed to similar treatment." This is a kind of application of the golden rule, and means that the mother-in-law ought to treat the daughter of another woman as she would like her own daughter to be treated by the mother-in-law in the house which she will enter as a bride. Such an appeal is the more forcible as the mother-in-law, in spite of her great authority in her own house over her son's bride, has little power of interfering in the interests of her daughter in the house belonging to her daughter's husband and his family. A Cujarathi proverb expresses this difference by declaring that "The mother-in-law in the house of her son is like a whale; in her daughter's house a cat." The daughter of the house seems to have an easier time than her married sister-in-law. "If the daughter walks it is like a mountain moving, if the daughter-in-law, it is waste of time," for, it is implied, the latter ought to be working. If the young bride commits any fault she cannot expect much indulgence, for "If the wife breaks anything it is an important thing, if the mother-in-law breaks anything it is a trifle." Under these circumstances it is no wonder that the mother-in-law is in Indian proverbs much what the cruel stepmother is in European and other fairy tales, so that the feelings of hatred towards her is expressed by saying that "The best of mothers-in-law is like a large boil," or less coarsely and directly by another proverb, which says that "However good a mother-in-law may be, she is, nevertheless, a mother-in-law." The daughter-in-law escapes from this oppressive rule, and, no doubt, herself becomes in turn an oppressor, when the mother-in-law either dies or is reduced to the condition of widowhood. For by this calamity even the all-powerful mother-in-law is reduced to impotence, and gives up the rule to her son and her son's wife. Her fall from her high estate of authority on the death of her husband is expressed in the strong language of the proverb, "When my husband lived, I was under a benevolent ruler; when the son succeeds to the throne I am under the rule of a boot." *Sic transit gloria mundi.*

Many other features of Indian domestic life are illustrated by proverbs. The native of India seems to have no doubt about the preferability of the married to the unmarried life. "Men with children," says a Cujarathi proverb, "are alone really men: unmarried men are like cattle," and again, "A house without children is like a burying-ground." The strength of maternal affection is indicated by two proverbs which say that "A mother's love is best of all," and "Anybody else but the mother will pierce a child's ear." The saying that "A mother that grinds the corn is better than a father of the rank of eight thousand," places the value of a mother's love far above the affection of a father, a judgment which is supported by the experience of all nations, and will not therefore lead us to imagine that the Indian father is in any way destitute of natural affection. It must, however, be noticed that parental affection, and especially paternal affection, in India would appear to be unequally distributed between sons and daughters. It is well known that the Hindus, like the Jews and the ancient Greeks, attach especial importance to their male offspring as necessary for the continuance of those sacrifices which secure the father's salvation after death. The comparative unimportance of female children is shown by the evidence of Indian sayings, and the former prevalence of female infanticide, to have in many cases quenched the natural feelings of parental affection. According to the proverbs, "A son is the lamp of a dark house," while "He that has a daughter is fined by God." Therefore when a daughter is unfortunately born, it is advisable to marry her and so get rid of her as soon as possible, for "A daughter grows up as fast as a dunghill," and "Goods for sale and a daughter in the house are best disposed of," the coarseness and brutality of which proverbs is, it may be remarked by the way, exceeded by the Scotch saying that "Daughters and deid fish are nae keepin' ware." The business of match-making is so zealously pursued by the parents that it is said "Nobody would run unless he had a daughter to dispose of." "A daughter and a cow should go where they are led," is a warning to the girl-child not to interfere with her parents' matrimonial plans. When married, the daughter is satisfactorily got rid of, for, whereas in England

> "My son's my son, till he get him a wife ;
> But my daughter's my daughter all the days of her life,"

in India "There is no more complete stranger in a house than the married daughter."

A large number of Indian proverbs refer to the ceremonies observed at marriage. Most of these festive ceremonies are dispensed with when the bride is a widow, as we might infer from the saying, "No drum at a widow's marriage, and no sugar in the kidgeree." At the same time there are certain substantial advantages in marrying a widow owing to the fact that even in the castes where re-marriage is allowed they are less in demand, so that the intending bridegroom has a larger supply to select from. This is expressed in the proverb, "When you want to marry a virgin, don't look about to choose; but when you have to marry a widow, pick and choose." Another proverb pretty distinctly recommends widows as wives, coupling them with such excellent specimens of their respective classes as Patels of Padra and horses of Sadra. If you want to marry riches, you are recommended to get "A daughter of Cujarat and a safe full of gold." The maternal uncle is an important person, as it is his duty in Cujarat to conduct the bridegroom to the place appointed for the marriage ceremony. Hence the Cujarathi equivalent for "Half a loaf is better than no bread," is, "He that hath no other uncle must put up with a squinting uncle." The bridegroom is not allowed to see his bride till the wedding day. She is chosen for him by a deputation of his relatives, upon whom a pretty deceit is sometimes practised by the family of the bride. "Ilai is shown and Jilai is made to sit upon the chair," that is, the best looking sister is exhibited to the party of inspection, and, when the wedding day comes, they find some inferior specimen of the family substituted in her place. Everybody is used to such a procedure in shopping. Ladies often complain that, when they have asked for a fine article exhibited at a low price in the window, the shopkeeper tries to palm off on them an inferior article from the stock in the shop. But it must be rather a trial to one's power of resignation to grin and bear the effects of a similar imposition in such an important matter as a marriage. When a wedding is arranged on principles of the strictest economy, it is said that "Neither were various vegetables, nor the wadi (imitation flowers) prepared, and the bride was got without money," and the same proverb is used in a wide sense as equivalent to our "Something for nothing." Generally speaking, "The nuptial procession is proportioned to the rank of the bridegroom." As to the happiness of Hindu married life we have already had evidence to show that the new bride is often unhappy owing to the oppression of her mother-in-law. Another severe thorn in the flesh is the presence of a co-wife, when the husband practises polygamy.

But most wives are free from this annoyance, as, except in exceptional cases, Hindus have to content themselves with single wives. When, however, for any reason the Hindu husband does take an extra wife, the result does not seem to be happy. Several proverbs in Mr. Roebuck's collection give strong negative evidence in favour of monogamy, and recognise the unhappiness produced by a plurality of wives. They inform us that "One wife is enough for a whole family," that "A fellow-wife, though a Houri, is worse than a she-devil," and that "The fellow-wife is intolerable even in effigy."

In India, as in medieval Europe, professional doctors found formidable rivals in old women looked up to for their experience and their knowledge of old established recipes. Aubrey tells us that Hobbes "was wont to say that he had rather have the advice or take physic from an experienced old woman that had been at many sick people's bedsides, than from the most learned but unexperienced physician." Bacon remarks in his *Advancement of Learning* that "empirics and old women are more happy many times in their cures than learned physicians," and attributes their success to the fact that they are more inclined to adhere to old medicines, the efficacy of which has been firmly established by experience, while physicians like to try new remedies. It is probably the same idea added to economical considerations that makes Indian proverbs speak of medicine as a profession that any stupid person who can do nothing else may without hesitation take up, while the saying that "An old woman in the house is a great assistance" may be regarded as a recognition of the value of experience unsupported by medical science At the same time in India as in England the existence of a certain number of proverbs and stories at the expense of doctors must not be regarded as indicating a general disbelief in the utility of medical science. Probably the originators of these stories are quite ready to call in the assistance of the doctor when they happen to fall ill. The ingratitude of people in health towards the doctors who cure them when they are sick, is noticeable all over the world, and is expressed clearly in two Indian proverbs, "A physician is an enemy when he has done his duty," and "Let the physician die when my disease is cured."

Besides the evidence on the subject of fondness for sugar mentioned above, other proverbs indicate native preferences for various articles of food. The height of luxury is "To eat plantains and ghee," which are fried together. Ghee is for cooking purposes much to be preferred to oil, as might be inferred from the proverb that "the family chaplain's pudding is cooked in oil, a stranger's in ghee." The most unpardonable mistake in Indian house-keeping is to put asafœtida into rice, for, as Mr. Roebuck informs the uninitiated, asafœtida should be put into split pease, and by no means into rice. Therefore when anyone makes a ridiculous mistake, it is said that "The woman has forgotten and put asafœtida into the rice." At Roman dinner parties it was a common practice to bring as uninvited guests friends who were called *umbrae* (shadows). The prevalence of the same practice in India is attested by such proverbs as "Three were invited and thirteen came; such is the custom here, the strangers eat up all, and the family may whistle for supper," and "One, I myself, the second my brother, the third the barber and shaver."

The Indian proverbs containing references to religion and the distinctions of caste are, as might be expected, very numerous. The sacredness of the great rivers of India is a well-known feature in the Hindu religion. Thus it is said that "All the stones of the Nerbudda are gods," and, if any blessing comes upon a person without effort on his part, the Ganges is said to flow into his house. The Indian equivalent of "What is everybody's business is nobody's business," will be found in "The mother of many children receives not the benefit of the Ganges." It is the son's duty to take his mother to the Ganges, but, as the fulfilment of this duty is often very expensive, it often happens that, when there are more sons than one, each is inclined to shift the burden upon the other, and so there is some danger of the duty remaining unperformed. The sacredness of the city of Benares is attested by a proverb which illustrates the greatest perverseness of fortune by the instance of a person who lived in Benares for twelve years and eventually died in Magadha, it being supposed, as Mr. Roebuck points out, that death in the latter city leads to transmigration into the form of an ass, while those who die in Benares obtain release from future birth. But it is not only rivers and cities that are sacred in India. The extreme sanctity of the cow is expressed by the proverb that "The cow feeds on grass, but even her tail is worshipped." The snake, too, comes in for a share of religious honour. The neglect of favourable opportunities when they come, and the consequent necessity of taking much trouble to find them at some subsequent period, is proverbially compared to the conduct of those who "do not worship the snake that comes to their house, but go to worship at his hole." Some trees also are sacred, for it is said that "If you rinse your mouth with the root of the jhil tree, your sin is washed away." *Jhil* is the Sindi name of the *Indigofera Pauciflora,* a tree out of which Hindu tooth-brushes are made. Naturally the Brahmins occupy a prominent position in Indian proverbs. As the Brahmins are in the habit of receiving gifts from everybody, it is the excess of impropriety to "ask a gift from a Brahmin." The absurdity of such a request could hardly be equalled, unless you were to "ask a Brahmin to kill a snake." As the Brahmins use leaves for platters and perform frequent ablutions, it is humorously said that "Water, stone, and leaves tremble at the sight of a Brahmin," and that "A Nagar is never black, and near a Brahmin's house there are no broad leaves." The Nagars are an exclusive caste of Brahmins in Cujarat, who no doubt pride themselves on their fair skins. However, the possibility of even a Brahmin flagrantly violating the rules of his caste and religion is contemplated by one proverb, which compares a person who, after taking solemn pledges, breaks them on the first opportunity, to a forgetful Brahmin who ate beef and swore never to eat it again. The strictness with which caste rules prevent men from leaving their own sphere is seen in the proverb that "A tailor's son must remain a tailor all his life." In other countries anyone may take a drink of water from anybody else. In India it is not so. The Hindu must, therefore, ascertain the caste of the person who offers him the draught before he ventures to drink. Therefore it is said that to drink water first and then ask the caste of the giver, is like giving your daughter away and then inquiring about the family. We must not leave the religious proverbs without giving a curious one referring to the worship of the goddess of small-pox and comparing a person who is ill-proportioned to "an offering to Sitla," the goddess of smallpox. Mr. Roebuck, in explaining this proverbial comparison, remarks that "it is customary with those who are seized with smallpox to make, after their recovery, votive offerings to the female deity who is supposed to preside over this disease, these consisting of figures in gold or silver, representing different parts of the body, as an eye, a nose, an ear, etc., which have been exempted from the effects of the disease." A similar practice prevails in a Roman Catholic church at Bandora near Bombay, where Goanese servants, who attribute the cure of any limb of their body to the intervention of the Virgin Mary, offer at her shrine a wax-work effigy of the part cured.

With the many proverbs referring to the ceremonial outward observances of religion must be contrasted others which express a revolt against exclusive attention to forms, and show a preference for virtuous conduct. In these we find some faint echoes of the scriptural denunciations against those Israelites who scrupulously performed sacrifices and observed fasts, but neglected the weightier matters of the law. One such proverb condemns the son "who disregards his living father and offers him the sraddha when he is dead," and another in a lofty spirit declares that "If the heart is pure, the Ganges will flow into one's katwat." The katwat is a vessel used by cobblers to hold water, and the proverb containing the word is said to have been first uttered by a poor cobbler whose poverty prevented him from travelling to the holy Ganges. The same idea is expressed more clearly, and at greater length, in a passage quoted by Professor Monier Williams, in his *Indian Wisdom*, from the *Mahabharata*:—

> "Triple restraint of thought and word and deed,
> Strict vow of silence, coil of matted hair,
> Close shaven head, garments of skin and bark,
> Keeping of fasts, ablutions, maintenance
> Of sacrificial fires, a hermit's life,
> Emaciation—these are all in vain,
> Unless the inward soul be free from stain."

There are also several proverbs condemning those whose conduct is inferior to their professions. Such are, "Men crushing fishes under their feet cry out Ram," and that which declares that "Religious principles properly belong to them who hold them in practice, and he bears a sword who uses it on the battle-field." Of distinctly immoral proverbs I have only noticed one. It is, according to my informant, derived from a Sanskrit origin, and is to the effect that "One should not care for the death of one's father, if a man has the choice and is thereby freed himself." Such immoral proverbs seem to be found in all languages, though they always form a very small minority when compared with the large number that inculcate religion and morality.

Some Hindu proverbs indicate a belief in there being a close connection between a man's character and his external appearance. Blackness of colour is looked upon with suspicion, though we are warned against regarding blackness as an infallible mark of villainy by an Indian equivalent of "All that glitters is not gold," which informs us that "All having very black skins are not the brothers-in-law of thieves." This contempt for black skins probably originated as early as the Aryan invasion of India, when the fairer skinned invaders from the north despised the blackness of the original natives as evidence of mental and moral inferiority. It is interesting to notice the same connection of ideas in the English language in such words as blackguard, blackleg, and in the combination of literal and metaphorical meaning in the English proverb, "The devil is not so black as he is painted." Another Indian proverb on the connection between looks and character lays down that "A short neck and low forehead are the marks of a bad disposition." The former part of this proverb agrees with the popular conception of a brutal prize-fighter as a person with a short and thick neck. But the idea of a low forehead indicating wickedness is not quite in accordance with English ideas, unless we assert invariable connection between intellectual and moral excellence. For in England a large brow is supposed to be the sign of intellectual power. When Keats calls Homer deep-browed he is attributing to him not moral goodness but poetic genius and mental power, and Tennyson is thinking of the narrow range of the savage intellect when, in *Locksley Hall*, he makes his hero scorn the idea of herding with narrow foreheads. Indian proverbial wisdom does not approve of beards. The proverb, "This beard is a screen for imposture," was probably a favourite jibe of the Hindus at what would appear to them to be the most characteristic feature in the personal appearance of their Mahometan conquerors. This idea of the usefulness of the beard for purposes of dissimulation is not a common one, but it is recognised by the great modern philosopher of Germany, who professes himself to be most in agreement with Indian philosophical and religious ideas, and would no doubt have been glad to have supported his opinion on the subject by the quotation of an Indian proverb. Schopenhauer supposes that the beard was given man to enable him to conceal his feelings. "The final cause of it," he remarks, "lies in the fact that the rapid alterations of the countenance betraying every movement of the mind are principally visible in the mouth and its vicinity: therefore in order to conceal these from the prying eye of the adversary as something dangerous in bargaining, or in sudden emergencies, nature gave man the beard. The woman, on the other hand, could dispense with this; for, with her, dissimulation and command of countenance are inborn." We must, of course, treat with respect the opinion of the profound Schopenhauer, but, at the same time, if we must search for the final cause of the beard, it seems more natural to think that the beard is more useful as a protection for a delicate throat than as an instrument of dissimulation.

As was noticed above, Indian proverbs taken as a whole give much the same generalizations from experience and rules for conduct as European proverbs. But they are expressed in different language, with a good deal of local colouring from the climate, the fauna, and the zoology, as well as from the manners and customs of this great peninsula. In this respect a large number of proverbs are characteristic of India, and could not have well originated in any other country. We often see a native of the country being shaved in the open air and gazing intently at the little mirror in his hands to see that the operation is performed to his satisfaction. The mirror is not his own but the barber's, and therefore anything that goes about from one person to another is "Like the barber's looking-glass in every one's hands." The rainy season on which the agricultural prosperity of the whole year depends will explain how failure is expressed by the question and answer, "If out of twelve months three are gone, what remains? Nothing," and also how the Indian equivalent for "Make hay while the sun shines" is "Wash your hands while the river is flowing." In Europe rivers are not usually looked upon as likely to dry up and cease flowing. The rustic of the Latin proverb, who sat down by the river bank to wait until the water flowed away and he could cross dry shod, might perhaps be regarded as a sensible person in the hot season of the year in India when great rivers dwindle away into tiny streams or entirely dry up. In England the principle of heredity is recognised by calling a man "a chip of the old block." The Indian says that "A son takes after his father as the fruit of a banyan is like the tree on which it grows." The preparations made to receive a great man on his travels in the villages through which he has to pass are alluded to in the proverbial address to an impudent boaster, "You don't know that you will be allowed to enter the town, yet you order the patel to have a warm bath ready." Sometimes Indian proverbs use fables as illustrations, like our European ideas of the basilisk killing with a look or of the ostrich hiding itself in the sand to conceal itself from the eyes of the hunter. In India there is a fiction that, when a musk-rat has been seized by a snake, the snake dies if he eats the musk-rat and becomes blind if he lets it go. Hence anyone who reduces another to a choice of evils is said to be "a musk-rat to a snake." The advisability of the cobbler sticking to his last is expressed in India by reference to an ambitious cobbler who went to Benares and got sawn in pieces. The fish that "fell out of the frying-pan into the fire" finds its Indian counterpart in the person who, "being troubled at home, went to the forest, and the forest took fire." "To dig a well when the house is on fire" is a good equivalent for our "Locking the door when the cow is out or when the steed is stolen." In India good things given to anyone who is unable to appreciate their excellence are compared not to "pearls before swine," but to sugar offered to an ass, which is one of the many proverbial expressions attesting the Hindu's love for sweet things. The Indian condemnation for a fool who rushes in where angels fear to tread is, "He knows not the charm even for a scorpion, and yet puts his hand into a snake's hole." The fact that the weakest goes to the wall is expressed by saying that "Whether the melon falls upon the knife, or the knife on the melon, the melon is the sufferer." Sometimes there is a close similarity not only in thought but also in words between Indian and English proverbs. Thus the Indian proverb that the mountains appear smooth, or, as it is sometimes given, beautiful in the distance, is almost the same, word for word, as the English proverb which Campbell expanded into :—

> "'Tis distance lends enchantment to the view,
> And clothes the mountains in their azure hue."

Proverbs have been defined as the wisdom of many and the wit of one. The proverbs of India, though equal in wisdom or prudence to those of Europe, seem, taken as a whole, to be rather deficient in wit. Yet sometimes we find in them very ingenious expressions of the truths to be conveyed. The almost magical advantage of union is pithily expressed by the proverb, "One and one makes eleven," because if you put 1 and 1 together the result is 11. It would be difficult to find an instance of more skilful use of metaphor than in this warning against quarrelling with friends:—"O Summun, do not rudely break the cord of friendship; if, after breaking, it should even be joined, a knot will remain." "Without being hammered a stone cannot become a god," is a powerful expression of the "uses of adversity," and the same truth seems to be enforced by an equally striking illustration in the proverb, "The trees bend when they bear fruit." But taking a general view of the subject, anyone who expects to find in Indian proverbs much subtlety, or masterly employment of language, will be disappointed. What they contain, except in a few exceptional cases, is a great amount of practical shrewdness expressed in homely words and illustrated by simple examples.

Indian and Homeric Epics.

THE Indian Epics are distinguished from all other Epics by their vastness and irregularity. The Iliad is one of the largest poems that Europe has ever produced, but the Ramayana is three times and the Mahabharata twelve times as long. The action of the Iliad is completed in fifty-one days, that of the Odyssey in forty days, while the two Indian Epics detail the events of many years. The vast Epic poems of India, in spite of their many beauties, must, when compared with the Iliad and Odyssey, suffer by the comparison, in like manner as the confused and often grotesque imagery depicted on the walls of Hindu temples, and the unhuman figures in their shrines, would appear barbarous and ugly if placed side by side with the frieze of the Parthenon or the statue of Athene. The Greeks living in a small country broken up by its mountains into many sub-divisions, where all was perfectly beautiful and limited in extent, early conceived an admiration for moderation as the true standard of excellence. Their philosophers regarded the limited as good and the unlimited as bad. In this spirit Aristotle determines that Babylon on account of its immense size could hardly be deemed worthy of the name of city, and that a poem should not be too long to be contemplated as a whole. Before this love of moderation obtained definite expression, as the guiding principle of philosophy and art, it was abundantly exemplified in Greek literature, and nowhere more conspicuously than in the Homeric Epics. In the Iliad and the Odyssey the heroes are superior indeed to ordinary men, but the greatest care is taken not to exaggerate their superiority beyond the range of possibility. Agamemnon is a mighty king, but the great army he leads to Troy is not larger than that which Pausanias commanded at Plataea. The shield of Achilles is described as being a wonderful work of art, and it would, no doubt, have been beyond the power of contemporary artists to represent all the pictures it contained, but that such a work is not beyond the power of art has been practically demonstrated in modern times by Flaxman. Diomede and Hector are stronger than average men, but their superiority is expressed in language of carefully guarded moderation. They are represented as lifting stones such as two ordinary men could not support. Virgil is less careful to observe the limits of possibility, and vainly tries to improve upon Homer and produce a greater effect upon his readers by making Turnus wield a stone which twelve men could scarcely carry. It would have been as easy to have given these heroes the strength of a hundred, a thousand, or even a million men, and an Indian poet would not have hesitated to prefer the larger to the smaller number as likely to be more impressive, forgetting that in many cases the part is more than the whole.

Such transgressions of the rule of the golden mean are continually committed by the Indian Epic poets. In the Ramayana and Mahabharata the reader is perfectly bewildered by the enormous numbers and hyperbolical descriptions intended to declare the prowess of the heroes. In the Iliad even the great goddess Athene contents herself with lifting up a landmark to hurl at Ares. Hanumat, in the Ramayana, tears up a great mountain by the roots and carries it through the air with the tigers, elephants, and gazelles that lived in large numbers on its slopes. He needs both hands to support the burden, but this does not prevent him from overcoming with his feet and his knees six powerful demons who attempt to oppose his progress. But even this is nothing to what he did before he picked up the mountain. Thirty million

Gandharvas had set upon him with clubs and swords, and he destroyed all those thirty million strong warriors in the twinkling of an eye. In one of the battles round Lanka the demon Indrajit in the eighth part of a day kills or wounds six hundred and forty millions of Rama's monkey allies. Such exploits cast far into the shade even the sway of the Archangel Michael's two-handed sword felling whole squadrons at once. In fact almost every exaggeration that occurs in other Epics may be found far outdone in the pages of the Ramayana and Mahabharata. In the Iliad the spear of Achilles passes right through the rim of Aeneas' shield, and, passing above his back, is fixed in the ground; and on another occasion Athene with her breath diverts Hector's spear, so that instead of striking Achilles it turns back and falls at its owner's feet. These two wonders are combined together and outdone by the arrow shot from Rama's bow, which, after passing through the heart of Ravana, came back of itself to the quiver when its work was accomplished. Witherington at Chevychase, fighting "on his stumps" when both his legs were cut off, is surpassed by the demon Kumbhakarna, who, after losing his arms and his feet, rushes open-mouthed upon Rama. None of the suitors in the Odyssey can bend the bow of Ulysses, even when they have tried to render it more supple by warming it before the fire and rubbing it with melted fat, but they can all lift it without any difficulty. Such a limited mark of a hero's prowess is far too little for the Ramayana. The bow which Rama has to pull is so big and heavy that it has to be brought in on an eight-wheeled hurdle drawn by five thousand men, and, not content with merely bending it, he breaks it asunder with such violence that all around hear a crash like that of a fallen mountain.

Whether there is any connection between the Indian and Greek Epics is a question not very easy to decide. Dion Chrysostom, a Greek writer belonging to the reign of Trajan, in a passage which evidently refers to the Ramayana and Mahabharata, speaks of these poems as Indian adaptations of the Iliad and Odyssey. His words are interesting as being the earliest record extant of the Indian Epic poems being introduced to Europeans, for it seems that Dion Chrysostom derived his information from the writings of Megasthenes, the friend of Seleucus Nicator, who at the end of the fourth century before Christ reigned over a kingdom which extended from the Euphrates to the Indus. This Megasthenes was sent as an ambassador to the capital of Sandracottus Chandra-gupta, king of the Prasii, which seems to have been somewhere near the modern city of Patna, and used well his opportunity of studying Indian manners and customs. It is from his writings, according to Professor Lassen, that Dion Chrysostom derived his information that "the poetry of Homer was said to be sung among the Indians transformed into their language and voice."

Is there any probability of this view being true, or is it merely one of the many instances showing the common Greek tendency to attribute a Greek origin to everything worthy of note to be found in foreign countries? It is certainly not historically impossible that the story of the Iliad and the Odyssey may have become known to the inhabitants of North-Western India before the fifth century. Greece and India had at that early date opportunities of influencing each other. Although there was little or no direct communication between the two countries, the Great Empire of Persia, which numbered among its subjects both Greeks and Indians, must occasionally have been the means of bringing them together, and afforded them the opportunity of exchanging ideas. Herodotus actually gives us an account of such a meeting, which is well worth quoting. "Darius," we are told, "after he had got the kingdom, called into his presence certain Greeks, who were at hand, and asked what he should pay them to eat their fathers when they died. To which they answered, that there was no sum that would tempt them to do such a thing. He then sent for certain Indians of the race called Callatians, men who eat their fathers, and asked them, while the Greeks stood by and knew by the help of an interpreter all that was said, what he should give them to burn the bodies of their fathers at their decease. The Indians exclaimed aloud and bade him forbear such language." If this interview ever took place, it must have been towards the end of the sixth or the beginning of the fifth century. When Xerxes succeeded his father we find that he led Indian sepoys to fight against Europeans, and thus anticipated the policy of the Malta expedition nearly twenty-four hundred years ago. These Indian auxiliaries entered Greece with Xerxes in the spring of 480, and did not return with him after the defeat of Salamis. Mardonius retained them all among the 300,000 picked troops with which he hoped to subdue Greece, so that they remained more than a year in the country, and took part in the battle of Plataea in the autumn of 479. Thus it came about that the Indians and Persians perished together on that fatal field, and the mingled dust of the ancestors of the modern Parsees and Hindus, who now live peaceably together in Bombay as subjects of Queen

Victoria, fertilised the rich plains of Bœotia. Just as Xerxes used Indian auxiliaries against Greece, Darius his father is almost certain to have employed Greek mercenaries when he conquered the Punjab. Some of them may have settled in the conquered country, and from them the natives of the country may have learnt the story of the Iliad and Odyssey. There is thus a probability of the Greeks having had intercourse with the Indians at about the time that the Ramayana is supposed to have been composed, and fragments of the Greek story may have penetrated from Darius' Indian province to the city of Bundelkhand, in which Valmiki, the author of the Ramayana, is said to have lived.

To this connection may be due the parallels that have been noticed between the Indian and Greek Epics. The great invasion of Ceylon described in the Ramayana is undertaken to recover Rama's wife, who has been carried away by Ravana. In like manner the object of the Trojan war is to restore to Menelaus his wife Helen, who had been carried away by Paris from Sparta. The siege of Lanka in the Ramayana is like a nightmare of the siege of Troy in the Iliad. A certain similarity in the incidents and sentiments forces itself upon any one who makes the comparison, however much it may be overlaid by the vast exaggerations of the Indian Epic. Both sieges are undertaken to recover a wife who has been stolen away from her husband. Sita suffers from the bitter abuse of the women in Lanka, just as Helen was attacked by her female relations in Troy. Sita also, like Helen, is inclined to be self-reproachful, only with this difference, that, being the type of a perfect woman in the life she was then living, and holding the Hindu doctrine of metempsychosis, she attributes her misfortunes to errors committed in a previous state of existence. When Hanumat, after the fall of Ravaṅa, beseeches Sita to be allowed to punish the women who had reviled her, as Ulysses punished the faithless servants of Penelope, she mercifully replies, "Let not the noble monkey be angry with servants forced to obey, who move according to the will of another. All that has come upon me by their doing I have endured as a punishment for the bad deeds I had done before, and by the fault of my adverse fortune. It is my destiny alone that had tied me to this wretched lot." The parallelism between Helen and Sita is further borne out by the resemblance between the thoughts aroused by those two heroines in the minds of those who were engaged in war on their account. In the celebrated scene of the Iliad painted by Zeuxis, Helen, when she appears on the Trojan walls, excites the admiration of the Trojan elders.

> "Helen they saw, as to the tow'r she came ;
> And ''tis no marvel,' one to other said,
> 'The valiant Trojans and the well-greav'd Greeks
> For beauty such as this should long endure
> The toils of war ; for goddess-like she seems.'"

Very similar are the thoughts of the monkeys when Sita, for whose release they have been fighting so long, is at last brought into their midst in a closed litter. They crowded round by thousands, desiring to see her, and said: "What sort of beauty does Sita possess? What a pearl among women must she be, for whose sake this world of monkeys underwent such great danger, for whose sake King Ravana, the monarch of demons, was killed, and a bridge one thousand miles long was built in the waters of the ocean?" In both passages great beauty is regarded as a sufficient justification for all the toil and danger that had been undergone. When Helen came to the tower she looked down on the plain below, and gave Priam a fine description of the various leaders of the Greek army. There seems to be a reminiscence of this striking description in another passage of the Ramayana. In the 6th book of that poem two spies who have returned from the camp of the besieging army go with Ravana to the top of his palace and point out to him the hostile leaders encamped in the plain beneath. Ravana, the demon king of Lanka, "with ten faces, copper-coloured eyes, a huge chest, and bright teeth like the new moon, tall as a mountain peak, stopping with his arms the sun and moon in their course, and preventing their rising," is at first sight utterly incomparable with the intensely human Hector, the defender of Troy. But in spite of the contrast the poet who tells the fall of Ravana might seem to have had in his mind the story of the Iliad, that may have come to his knowledge in a more or less distorted form. Ravana, like Hector is represented as being utterly merciless in the field of battle, but when he appears in private life we are surprised to find him chivalrously polite to his loving wife, whose fears for his safety remind us of Andromache's similar anxiety in the 6th Iliad. She advises him to send Sita to Rama's camp accompanied with precious gifts, and he replies courteously, with an expression of the same sentiment as Hector utters in answer to Andromache's similar appeal, that, if he refused to do battle with his adversaries, he would be disgraced in the eyes of all, and that life would not be worth living, if he so forfeited his high reputation. In his last great battle he eventually discovers, like Hector, that the fates are against him and he must die, but though conscious of this he does not abate his resolution to fight out the battle to the bitter end. When his horse wept large tears and thunder from a cloudless sky portended his destruction, he bravely bore up against his evil destiny. "I must conquer," said Rama; "I must die," said Ravana. This consciousness of coming death is present with Hector also at his last hour, when, deserted by God and man, he rushes desperately at Achilles, exclaiming:—

> "Oh Heav'ns! the Gods above have doom'd my death!
> Now is my death at hand, nor far away:
> Escape is none; since so hath Jove decreed,
> And Jove's far-darting son, who heretofore
> Have been my guards; my fate hath found me now.
> Yet not without a struggle let me die
> Nor all inglorious; but let some great act,
> Which future days may hear of, mark my fall."

Finally the catastrophe of the poems is brought about by the death of Ravana, who, after being lamented by his wives with lamentations like those of Hecuba, Andromache, and Helen, is, by the permission of his enemy, burned on the funeral pyre with obsequies closely resembling the honours paid to dead Hector in the end of the Iliad.

The Ramayana reminds us most of the Iliad from the general resemblance of the main events in the two poems. Occasionally, however, we seem to find also recollections of Homer in the sentiment expressed. Sarpedon's celebrated speech in the 12th Iliad begins by insisting on the fact expressed by the French proverb "*noblesse oblige*," and goes on to declare that the certainty of death should make men prefer glory to length of days. The Lycian king first shows that kings having higher privileges and greater honour than ordinary men are bound to show a corresponding superiority in labour and courage. Then he goes on to say that as death must come soon or late, it may be met honourably rather than dishonourably avoided :—

> "O friend ! if we, survivors of this war,
> Could live, from age and death for ever free,
> Thou shouldst not see me foremost in the fight,
> Nor would I urge thee to the glorious field :
> But since on man ten thousand forms of death
> Attend, which none may 'scape, then on, that we
> May glory on others gain, or they on us."

Both the leading thoughts of this fine speech may be found clearly expressed in the reproaches uttered by Angada against the monkeys fleeing before Kumbhakarna. "Where go ye now," he says, "frightened like ignoble monkeys forgetful of yourselves, your valour, and your race ? Come, turn back. Wherefore do you wish to save your lives? By fleeing whither, do you think you can evade death, valiant Vanari? Since death is ordained of necessity, it is better for people like you to die in battle. To obtain life or death is not in your power. Therefore preferring to everything the duty of warriors, fight, illustrious Vanari." Again in another passage Hanumat says, "Flight is unbecoming in heroes of noble race," repeating one of the ideas that occur in Sarpedon's speech quoted above.

Besides the resemblances already referred to, we may notice that Ravana deludes the besieging army with a magical image of Sita, just as Apollo deceives the Greeks by bringing into battle a figure representing Aeneas. In the Ramayana, as in the Iliad, slaughter is foreboded by the falling of bloody rain. Ravana's horses weep before the death of Ravana, just as the horses of Achilles do after Patroclus has fallen. Vibhishina proposes that noble ladies should prepare the bath for Rama and anoint him with perfumes, just as the attendant ladies of Helen bathe and anoint Pisistratus and Telemachus when they visit Menelaus. The brilliancy of the palace of Menelaus in Lacedaemon is compared to the brightness of the sun, and the brilliancy of Ravana's palace in Lanka is illustrated by the same comparison. Those who support the unity of authorship of the Iliad and Odyssey quote, among other parallel passages, in support of their view, the fact that the speed of the Phaeacian ships is compared to the speed of thought, and that the same comparison is found in a more elaborate form in the Iliad. In the Ramayana we more than once find this simile used to illustrate the speed of horses. In the Odyssey the Phaeacian ships are said to move without rudders in accordance with the will of the sailors, and in like manner in the Ramayana the chariot of Indra is represented as moving voluntarily in obedience to the will of the charioteer. Doubtless many other parallel passages would be discovered if any one perfectly acquainted with both sides of the comparison subjected the Ramayana to a searching examination side by side with the Homeric poems. But enough has been said to show that it is not at all impossible that Megasthenes may have been right in supposing that the Ramayana owed something to the Homeric poems.

If we now turn from the Ramayana to the more immense Mahabharata, we find less similarity to the Homeric poems in the framework of the poem and more in the details. The winning of Draupadi in the Mahabharata very closely resembles the bow-scene in the Odyssey. In the latter poem

Penelope promises to marry whichever of the suitors can bend Ulysses' bow. All the suitors fail, and then, in spite of their indignant murmurs, Ulysses in his beggar's rags bends the bow and shoots the arrow through a row of axeheads. In the Mahabharata, Draupada promises his daughter Draupadi to whoever will bend an enormous bow and shoot five arrows simultaneously through a revolving ring to hit a target beyond. Arjuna is present in the coarse dress of a mendicant Brahmin, and in spite of the indignation of the suitors, performs the feat. In the battles of the Mahabharata we are chiefly concerned with human warriors, and are no longer bewildered by the millions of monkeys and demons that slaughter each other round the walls of Lanka. But probability is violated, and the human interest of the struggle is decreased, in the Mahabharata also by immense exaggerations, which appear still more monstrous as the actors are represented as being ordinary men. It would be tedious to enumerate in detail the wonderful exploits performed by the heroes on either side. Professor Monier Williams says with truth that "when Arjuna is described as killing five hundred warriors simultaneously, or as covering the whole plain with dead and filling rivers with blood; Yudhishthira, as slaughtering a hundred men in a mere twinkle;

Bhima, as annihilating a monstrous elephant, including all mounted upon it, and fourteen foot soldiers besides, with one blow of his club; Nakula and Sahadeva, fighting from their chariots, as cutting off heads by the thousand and sowing them like seed upon the ground,—we at once perceive that the utter unreality of such scenes mars the beauty of the description." The story of Bhishma's fall is a good instance to show what extreme forms such hyperbolical descriptions may take. He is represented as being transfixed by so many arrows that when he falls from his chariot his body cannot touch the ground. For such instances as these no parallels could be found among the battles of the god-like men and man-like gods who fought in the plains of Troy. Achilles at his best can only kill one man at a time, and no hero on the Trojan plains is represented as bristling with the javelins that have pierced his side. I doubt whether any such instance of exaggeration could be found in any Greek or Roman Epics, until the time of the silver age, when a close parallel to this description is found in Lucan's Pharsalia. There Scaeva, the defender of Cæsar's camp, is represented as pierced by so many wounds that "nothing now defends his naked vitals except the spears sticking on the surface of his bones."

Still, although such extravagant incidents do not disfigure the pages of the Iliad, in some respects these unearthly battles do remind us of the Trojan war. There is, at any rate, one striking peculiarity common to the Greek and Indian Epics. The use of cavalry in war, familiar as it is in the historical periods of Greece and India, is as conspicuous by its absence in the Mahabharata and the Ramayana as in the Iliad and the Odyssey. The chief heroes in the Pandava and Kuru armies fight never on horseback but on chariots generally drawn by two horses, and each hero is supported by a charioteer, who is often a person of great importance, being generally the next in power to the prince who fights on the chariot. Even the gods sometimes perform this office for their favourites. Thus Krishna drives Arjuna's chariot, just as the goddess Athene drives that of Diomede. We may also notice that in the Iliad it is a very common device on the part of the poet to give a kind of partial triumph to a hero by allowing him to kill, not the adversary he actually aims at, but the charioteer driving his adversary's chariot. This particular casualty is twice mentioned as taking place in the first day's battle of the Mahabharata. In fact the whole account of this first battle is very spirited, and reads occasionally like an extract from the Iliad, being free from the exaggeration which mars, at any rate in European eyes, the interest of some of the other battle pieces in the Indian Epics. In it, as in the 11th Iliad, a shower of blood falls upon the field as a presage of the coming horrors. Karna, leading the van of the Kuru host, advanced

> "Gorgeous, shining as the rising sun ;
> His warriors deemed the gods themselves were weak
> With Indra at their head to stem his prowess,"

which, though more exaggerated, is very like the language in which the poet of the Iliad extols the prowess of Hector, when he burst the gate of the Greek camp, and "no one," in the words of the Iliad, "without the gods could have stemmed his onset."

Arjuna's last charge in the same battle, when

> "On he dashed with whirring wheel
> Through the deep streams of blood with carcases
> And shattered weapons choked, and thundering drove
> Against the Kuru ranks,"

reads very like the description in the 11th book of how Hector's horses bore

> "The flying car, o'er corpses of the slain
> And broken bucklers trampling ; all beneath
> Was plash'd with blood the axle, and the rails

Around the car, as from the horses' feet
And from the felloes of the wheels were thrown
The bloody gouts ; yet on he sped to join
The strife of men and break the opposing ranks."

In the passage of arms at Hastinapura, Kripa asks Karna his parentage, to see if he is of high enough birth to engage in combat with Arjuna. The description of Karna's demeanour, when being asked the question and unable to answer he

"silent stood
And hung his head, as when surcharged with dew
The drooping Lotus bows its fragrant blossom,"

irresistibly reminds us of a passage in the Iliad, which Virgil afterwards imitated :—

" Down sank his head, as in a garden sinks
A ripened poppy charged with vernal rains.
So sank his head beneath the helmet's weight." [1]

These striking parallels, all except the last of which are taken from Wilson's translation of the account of the first day's battle, may be taken as

[1] *cf.* Inque humeros cervix collapsa recumbit.
Purpureus veluti quum flos succisus aratr'
Languescit moriens, lassove papavera collo
Demisere caput pluvia quum forte gravantur.
Aen. ix. 432.

specimens of the considerable likeness which exists between the Iliad and the Mahabharata. Their number could be largely increased by taking a survey of the whole fighting portion of the great Indian Epic. Although, together with the resemblances noticed in the Ramayana, they might possibly be attributed, if no other alternative were possible, partly to similarity of subject, partly to the common origin of the Greeks and Indians, and the consequent similarity of manners and customs that remained until the advance of civilisation and difference of climate and other circumstances had begun to obliterate their original resemblance, it seems more natural to account for them by the indirect connexion between Indians and Greeks that must, as we have seen, have existed in the beginning of the fifth century before Christ.

Morality of the Mahabharata.

It has often been remarked that, whereas science has made immense strides since the early days of Greek philosophy, metaphysics and moral philosophy have remained stationary, so that modern philosophers, though in different terms, now discuss the very same problems as occupied the minds of Plato and Aristotle, and are no nearer their solution. An examination of Sanskrit literature shows that the unprogressive character of metaphysics and ethics may be still further illustrated. Berkeley's ideal theory was held by the later Vedanta school many centuries before Bishop Berkeley was born. Sanskrit philosophers, such as Kanada and Charvaka, at a very early age discovered for themselves atomism, materialism, and many other logical and metaphysical doctrines that have been vigorously defended and opposed again and again by successive generations of European philosophers. Schopenhauer, whose philosophy is believed by many to be the philosophy of the future, in spite of the lapse of time that intervened between himself and them, thought that the ancient philosophers of India, together with Plato and Kant, saw more deeply into the nature of things than any other of his predecessors. Exhaustively to detail all the parallelism existing between Indian and European philosophy would be almost the labour of a lifetime. It is possible, however, to get a few definite ideas on the subject by confining our attention to a limited portion of Sanskrit literature and a limited portion of the whole range of philosophy.

An examination of the moral philosophy contained in the *Mahabharata* would show that the author or authors of that great epic had clearly thought out some of the most important questions that are now discussed by modern moralists. Professor Monier Williams has collected, in his *Indian Wisdom*, a number of moral precepts out of the *Mahabharata*, which certainly testify to the very high morality of the writers. It is not, however, fair to regard them as average specimens of the morality of this immense poem. The *Mahabharata*, a poem or collection of poems twelve times as large as the *Iliad*, and the work of different authors, is composed of nobler and baser materials. A careful selection of the most exalted sentiments it contains, unless taken side by side with such other passages as are in conflict with our ideas of right and wrong, would give a misleading idea of the general moral atmosphere of the poem. We must remember that several very base deeds are ascribed to the heroes, and even to those gods who take a prominent part in the action. The five human heroes of the poem are the sons of Pandu, who are collectively represented as being far superior in virtue to their enemies the Kauravas. The eldest of the five is held up to our admiration as a pattern of perfect virtue, while the other four, though not represented as free from failings, are evidently intended to be heroic in character. Yet we find that they are all married to one wife like the ancient Britons, or the Todas on the Neilgherry Hills, among whom polyandry is still practised. Such a union is opposed to the moral sentiments of all civilised nations in the East as well as the West. In the rest of the conduct of the five Pandavas we find a good deal that is opposed to our ideas of what ought to be. Perhaps the worst act told of them in the *Mahabharata* is the story of the burning house. The five Pandavas, with their mother, were invited by their enemies to a house, which was built of inflammable materials, in order that it might be burnt over their heads. Hearing of the plot, they got an underground passage made, so that they might be able to escape when the house was set on fire. One night an outcast woman with her five children came to receive charity from the Pandavas. They drank till they were unconscious, and lay down in the house oppressed with sleep and wine. Then Bhima himself set fire to the house, and escaped with his four brothers and mother by the underground passage, leaving the outcast woman and her five children to their fate. They were burnt alive, and their charred corpses were mistaken for the bodies of the Pandavas, which was so convenient that it looks as if they had been left behind on purpose to conceal their flight. At any rate, Bhima and his brothers seem not to have had the least concern for the six innocent persons that they left to perish by a horrible death.

When we examine the characters of the five brothers separately, we find that several of their actions are so bad that their being attributed to the heroes of the poem must have a bad moral effect on those who try to find in it heroic examples for their guidance in life. Even the otherwise perfect Yudhishthira's character is marred by reckless gambling and a tendency to cowardice. As a gambler, he pledged his kingdom, his brothers, himself, and even his wife. His cowardice is shown on one occasion when he flies before Drona on a fleet horse, and on another when he sends his nephew, a boy of sixteen years, to almost certain death, instead of going himself on the dangerous enterprise. Bhima, the second brother, disgraces himself by many acts of ferocity, such as could scarcely be paralleled in the actions of the heroes of any European fictions. In the *Iliad*, Achilles exclaims in his fury that he would like to eat the flesh of his enemy, Hector, but never really thinks of doing so. In the *Mahabharata*, Bhima, after cutting off the head of his enemy, Duhsasana, catches the blood in his two hands and actually drinks it up, exclaiming, "Ho! ho! Never did I taste anything in the world so sweet as this blood." Again, in his fight with Duryodhana, he strikes his enemy with his mace on the thigh, which in a combat with the mace is considered to be foul play. The base blow breaks Duryodhana's thigh and brings him to the ground, whereupon Bhima brutally kicks his fallen enemy on the head. Such acts as these cannot be justified even by consideration of the deadly insults they were intended to avenge. Arjuna, who, according to Professor Monier Williams, "may be regarded as the real hero of the *Mahabharata*, of undaunted bravery, generous, with refined and delicate sensibilities, tender-hearted, forgiving, and affectionate as a woman, yet of superhuman strength, and matchless in arms and athletic exercises," nevertheless takes an unfair advantage of Karna, when that hero is trying to disengage his chariot wheel. He also gives the hint to Bhima, suggesting that he should use foul play and strike Duryodhana on the thigh.

Both these base actions of the two younger Pandavas are, strange to say, suggested by the god Krishna, who also suggested the following extraordinary prevarication to effect the death of the formidable Drona. Krishna advised Yudhishthira to tell a lie to Drona, and falsely inform him that his son Aswatthama was dead, in order that grief might make him throw down his arms. This the virtuous Yudhishthira refused to do. Krishna then found a way out of the difficulty by getting an elephant called Aswatthama killed. Bhima, killed the elephant and told Drona that Aswatthama was dead. Drona would not believe Bhima and asked Yudhishthira, whose reputation for virtue was a sufficient guarantee that he would speak the truth, whether his son was really dead. Yudhishthira, in answer to the question, said, "Aswatthama is dead; not indeed the man, but the elephant." But Krishna and Arjuna made such a noise directly Yudhishthira had said "Aswatthama is dead," that Drona could not hear the following words. This incident shows Bhima, Krishna, and even Arjuna, who is represented in the poem as a man who never told a lie, all joining in a mean prevarication. Even Yudhishthira's conduct is a little suspicious in the matter. It must in fairness be acknowledged, that some of the deviations from ordinary morality, which mar the characters of the heroes of the *Mahabharata*, do not pass uncondemned in the poem itself. Thus Yudhishthira has to do penance in hell for the deceit practised on Drona, and himself strikes his brother Bhima in the face as a punishment for the base blow he dealt in his combat with Duryodhana. But very many bad acts are narrated without either praise or blame, as if they did not at all detract from the heroism of the actors.

But if we find in some of the actions ascribed to the heroes a very low ideal of morality, throughout the poem, in the sentiments expressed, we have wonderful anticipations of the highest precepts of European religion and philosophy. Some of the most remarkable of these moral sentiments, culled from various portions of the *Ramayana* and *Mahabharata*, may be found translated into blank verse by Professor Monier Williams in his *Indian Wisdom.*

> "Do naught to others which if done to thee
> Would cause thee pain; this is the sum of duty,"
> (*Mahabharata* v. 1537,)

is an anticipation not only of the golden rule of Christianity, but also of the categorical imperative of Kant, that bids us only act on a rule that we could will to be law universal.

> "Bear railing words with patience, never meet
> An angry man with anger, nor return
> Reviling for reviling, smite not him
> Who smites thee: let thy speech and acts be gentle,"
> (*Mahabharata* v. 1270,)

is a passage that reminds us of Socrates' assertion that it is better to suffer than inflict injustice, and still more of the words of Christ, Luke vi. 27-29.

> "Just heaven is not pleased with costly gifts,
> Offered in hope of future recompense,
> As with the merest trifles set apart
> From honest gains, and sanctified by faith,"
> (*Mahabharata* xiv. 2788,)

is the same truth as Christ inculcated when He called the attention of His disciples to the contrast between the rich men offering costly gifts out of their abundance, and the poor widow who, out of her want, cast in her two mites, all that she had, even all her living. There are about fifty similar extracts from the *Mahabharata* quoted by Professor Monier Williams, most of which are in the same high strain, inculcating a far more advanced morality than is to be found anywhere in the literature of Greece and Rome, except in the works of one or two professed moral philosophers.

Although the *Mahabharata* is popularly ascribed to one author called Vyasa, it is believed by Sanskrit scholars to have really been the work of several centuries from 500 B.C. to the second or third century of our era. This theory would of course give an easy explanation of the divergence of moral sentiment to be found in different parts of the poem. Only a very wide interval of time between the most ancient and most modern portions of the *Mahabharata* could account for its containing, together with a style of fighting more brutal than any to be found in the *Iliad* and *Odyssey*, moral sentiments rivalling the most spiritual utterances of Seneca, Epictetus, and Marcus Aurelius in their resemblance to the doctrines of Christianity. It is, therefore, almost certain that the original foundation of the whole structure was the narrative describing the gambling, the exile, and the great war, and that writers of subsequent centuries, when civilisation had improved morality and introduced intellectual speculation, added numerous philosophical disquisitions to the original epic. It is even thought by some scholars that the striking parallels between the *Mahabharata* and Christianity may be due to late interpolations made after the influence of Christianity and some knowledge of Christian doctrines had permeated to India. But the difficulty of determining even approximately the date of the various portions of the poem is so great, that it seems better to look upon it as one whole representing the state of civilisation that prevailed in India during the ages of Greek and Roman history. By surveying it in this light we can at least determine how much brutality prevailed in the most barbarous, which was probably the earliest, epoch of this period, and also what an advance in moral and metaphysical philosophy had been made before the *Mahabharata* took its present form.

Such metaphysical speculations as occur in the *Bhagavadgita* and elsewhere we have not space to examine. It is easier to confine ourselves to the ethical element in the poem. That Sanskrit moralists had worked out independently the moral conclusions that are often supposed to be the peculiar property of European thinkers, may be clearly seen from an ethical argument given in the third book of the *Mahabharata.* Pratap Chandra Roy, the Secretary of the Datavya Bharata Karyalaya, who is devoting himself to the laborious task of translating the whole *Mahabharata* literally into English prose, has proceeded so far in his great work, that a considerable portion of the *Mahabharata* is now accessible to all the English speaking world. As the part already translated includes the third book, we can quote from Pratap Chandra Roy's work the very words used in the discussion we have to examine. The persons who take part in the dialogue are Yudhishthira, his brother Bhima, and their common wife Draupadi. Yudhishthira had lost in a gambling match with his cousin Duryodhana his kingdom, his own liberty, the liberty of his four brothers, and finally his wife Draupadi. Duryodhana and one of his brothers in the exultation of their triumph submitted Draupadi, whom they claimed as a slave in accordance with the result of their gambling, to terrible insults and indignities. But the father of Duryodhana would not allow Yudhishthira to surrender the kingdom he had lost, and sent him with his brothers and their wife Draupadi back to their capital city. Duryodhana pointed out to his father the impolicy of this concession, and besought that he might at least be allowed to play another gambling match with Yudhishthira, on the understanding that the loser with his brothers should go into exile for thirteen years. This was permitted, and Yudhishthira, who lost again, went with his four brothers and Draupadi to spend their years of exile in the forest. Bhima and Draupadi try to persuade Yudhishthira that he ought not to wait the stipulated thirteen years, but take immediate vengeance on their enemies for the indignities they have suffered. But their arguments are answered from a higher level of morality by Yudhishthira, who is intended to be the embodiment of perfect virtue. For Yudhishthira was the son of the God of Justice, and, as soon as he was born, an incorporeal voice said, "This child shall be the best of men—the foremost of those that are virtuous. Endowed with great prowess and truthful in speech, he shall certainly be the ruler of the Earth. Possessed of prowess and honesty of disposition, he shall be a famous king known throughout the three worlds." Accordingly, just as the speeches of Christ in *Paradise Regained*, of Æneas in the *Æneid*, and of King Arthur in the *Idylls of the King* may be assumed to represent the opinions of Milton, Virgil, and Tennyson, so the sentiments uttered by Yudhishthira are intended to give expression to the highest moral sentiments of the authors of the *Mahabharata,* while any opinions that he contests are thereby condemned as wrong.

Apart from religious considerations, there are, as Mr. Sidgwick shows in his *Methods of Ethics,* three ultimate reasons which are supposed to justify conduct and show its reasonableness. If a man is asked why he refuses to make himself wealthy by appropriating trust money, he may reply that such an action would make him liable to punishment, or that it would cause unhappiness both to the person deprived of his property and also to the world generally, owing to the feeling of insecurity and mistrust engendered by such acts, or finally that he sees clearly without regard to consequences that it is his duty not to do such an action. The first answer is egoistic, the second utilitarian, and the third may be called intuitional. If a man were always to guide his conduct by considerations of self-interest, he would be a consistent egoist; if he always aimed at general happiness, he would be a consistent utilitarian; if he always acted in accordance with his intuitions of right and wrong without regarding consequences, he would be a consistent intuitionist. As a matter of fact, most men waver between these three ultimate reasons, sometimes appealing to one, and sometimes to another, and not recognising the possibility of a conflict, and therefore not seeing any necessity to determine which of the three is superior to the others. We shall see that all three principles are clearly appealed to in the dialogue under consideration, and that Yudhishthira declares in favour of the strictest form of intuitionism as affording the true standard of action.

Draupadi, at the commencement of the dialogue which we wish to examine, calls upon Yudhishthira not to forgive the Kauravas, but to take vengeance upon them. She quotes an old sage, who showed on egoistic principles the evils of continual forgiveness, and also the evils of continually punishing every offence. There is a time for forgiveness and a time for punishment. "He that becometh forgiving at the proper time, and harsh and mighty also at the proper time, obtaineth happiness both in this world and the other." She finishes her appeal by urging that the case of the insolent treatment they have received from the Kauravas is not a proper occasion for forgiveness, but requires immediate vengeance.

In his first reply to Draupadi, Yudhishthira confines himself for the most part to egoistic and utilitarian considerations. Although these principles are not the sole justification of his conduct, he can quite reasonably employ them as arguments against a person who had argued against forgiveness on egoistic grounds. Thus opposing egoistic arguments by other egoistic arguments he finds a common ground with his antagonist. The reply may be partly regarded as an *argumentum ad hominem*, but it also has a certain amount of absolute force, as egoistic considerations are generally acknowledged to be reasonable in themselves, however inferior in importance to the higher interests with which they may conflict. Yudhishthira first shows how anger leads to all kind of sin. "The angry man committeth sin; the angry man killeth even his preceptors. The angry man insulteth even his superiors in harsh words. The man that is angry faileth to distinguish between what should be said and what should not. There is no act that an angry man may not do, no word that an angry man may not utter. From anger a man may slay one that deserveth not to be slain, and may worship one that deserveth to be slain. The angry man may even send his own soul to the regions of Yama." So far the argument appears to be intuitional, since it condemns anger as productive of injustice and other vices. But when Yudhishthira goes on to say that the wise, beholding all this, control their anger, desirous of obtaining high prosperity both in this and the other world, the ultimate reason furnishing the basis of the argument is seen to be the egoistic principle that it is reasonable for each man to secure his own prosperity, and his remark that truth is more beneficial than untruth, and gentle than cruel behaviour, appears from the context to be rather egoistic than utilitarian. At the same time it is apparently recognised by the speaker that either anger or some substitute for anger is necessary to protect the individual against wrong and as a check upon evil doing. The usefulness of resentment has been abundantly shown by Bishop Butler and other moralists. It will be generally allowed that if anger disappeared from the world and nothing took its place, an appalling increase of wickedness would be the result, as evil doers would fear no punishment. Is there then any means by which anger and its evil effects could be banished from the world without its good effects being lost at the same time? Yudhishthira suggests an escape from this difficulty, which he seems to have vaguely discerned. He says that "they that are regarded by the learned of foresight, as possessed of (true) force of character, are certainly those who are wrathful in outward show only." This seems to suggest that, when we suffer wrong, we should not allow ourselves to be driven to rash acts of punishment by gusts of passion, but should appear to be angry and act as if we were angry, in order that the injustice may not be repeated. This is an ingenious suggestion, but it is to be feared that ordinary men, without the stimulus of real indignation, would not, in cold blood, take the trouble to punish evildoers. The reply to Draupadi then goes on to take rather a utilitarian character. It is argued that if wrathful requital became law universal, the continuance of life would be impossible. "If the injured return their injuries, if one chastised by his superiors were to chastise his superiors in return, the consequence would be the destruction of every creature. . . . If the king giveth way to wrath, his subjects soon meet with destruction. Wrath, therefore, hath for its consequence the destruction and the distress of the people." Thus wrath is condemned as incompatible with the happiness and the continued existence of living creatures. The end of this section of the Vana Parva reverts to egoistic considerations of the state of bliss to be obtained by the forgiving in another world.

Draupadi answers Yudhishthira's egoistic arguments by pointing to the fact that the wicked sometimes flourish while the virtuous are unfortunate. As an instance she gives Yudhishthira himself, who regarded virtue as dearer than life, and was nevertheless robbed of his kingdom and driven into exile, while his wicked cousins enjoyed prosperity.

Yudhishthira might have answered her on egoistic grounds by declaring that happiness is by no means entirely to be identified with outward prosperity, and that he in exile under the foliage of the Dwaitavana forest was really happier than Duryodhana in his palace. Whether the poet thought of such a reply or not, he makes Yudhishthira take a different and a higher ground. Kant, the strictest of modern moralists, teaches that no act is really virtuous, unless it is formally virtuous, that is, unless it is done simply from love of duty. If any other motive of natural inclination leads to the action, however much it may outwardly resemble a virtuous action, it is not really virtuous. This very strict criterion of moral action is anticipated in the *Mahabharata* by Yudhishthira, who says to Draupadi, "I never act, solicitous of the fruits of my actions! I give away, because it is my duty to give; I sacrifice, because it is my duty to sacrifice! My heart is naturally attracted towards virtue. The man who wisheth to reap the fruits of virtue is a trader in virtue. His nature is mean, and he should never be counted among the virtuous." He then goes on further to show that the man who does an act outwardly virtuous from desire of reward not only fails to be virtuous, but also loses the reward he expected for his seeming virtue, thus by his folly sacrificing happiness both in this world and the next.

Draupadi's reply is rather incoherent. Indeed she declares herself to be raving. In her previous speech she had advocated fatalism: in this she insists upon the freedom of the will. She uses one favourite modern argument in support of freedom. "It is," she says, "because a person is himself the cause of his work that he is applauded when he achieveth success. So the doer is censured if he faileth. If man were not himself the cause of his acts, how could all this be justified." This argument is strongly stated. It can only be answered by denying entirely the justice of reward and punishment, and saying that reward and punishment, though unjust, may be reasonably inflicted on grounds of expediency. Thus the freedom of the will is based on the possibility of justice. Draupadi appeals to the freedom of the will as proving that prosperity may be secured by action, and therefore urges her husband to make an energetic attempt to recover his kingdom. Such an argument is of course a very inconclusive reply to

Yudhishthira's perfectly disinterested profession of virtue.

The next speaker in the dialogue is Bhima, the most impetuous of the five brothers. "Why," he exclaims, "in obedience to the trite merit of sticking to a promise, dost thou suffer such distress, abandoning that wealth which is the source of both virtue and enjoyments? . . . That virtue, which tortureth one's own self and friends, is really no virtue. It is rather a vice producing calamities. . . . He that practiseth virtue for virtue's sake always suffereth. He can scarcely be called a wise man, for he knoweth not the purposes of virtue, like a blind man incapable of perceiving the solar light." Bhima throughout his speech regards virtue as a means to the attainment of happiness, and as being on a par with wealth and pleasure. "One should not devote oneself to virtue alone," he says, "nor regard wealth as the highest object of his wishes, nor pleasure, but should ever pursue all three." In conclusion he urges his brother to cultivate the virtues of the warlike caste to which he belongs, and recover his kingdom by force of arms. Even sins committed in gaining a kingdom, he adds, can easily be expiated by sacrifices and bountiful gifts to Brahmins. Yudhishthira, in reply, maintains that the promise given before the gambling match, that if he lost he would retire with his brother for thirteen years, was a binding engagement which he could not break for the sake of an earthly kingdom. He ends by saying, "I regard virtue as superior to life itself and a blessed state of celestial existence. Kingdom, sons, fame, wealth—all these do not come up to even a sixteenth part of truth."

Bhima once more calls for immediate vengeance, passionately exclaiming, that "if a man slaying his injurer goeth the very day into hell, that hell becometh heaven to him." Then Yudhishthira changes his line of argument, perhaps despairing of exciting in the breasts of his hearers his own disinterested love of virtue, and points out to Bhima the immense difficulties that will have to be overcome if they rashly, without much deliberation, rush to battle with their enemies.

All through the argument dramatic discrimination of character has been well maintained. Draupadi, like a woman, shifts her ground and is prevented by her strong emotions from rigidly maintaining her line of argument. The hot-headed Bhima gives forcible expression to his comparatively low moral sentiments. Yudhishthira, in accordance with his repution for virtue, acknowledges humbly the justice of the reproaches, to which he has subjected himself by his unhappy gambling, but never swerves in his determination to abide by his plighted word, whatever may be the consequences, although at the same time he shows that honesty is really the best policy. Thus it may be concluded that the writer of the *Mahabharata*, or of this part of it, while recognising the importance of egoistic and utilitarian considerations to guide others in the way of virtue, had himself adopted a system of intuitionism closely resembling Kant's.

THE END.

Printed by Cowan & Co., Limited, Perth.